Why Did I Do It Again?

Understanding My Cycle of Problem Behaviors

a guided workbook for clients in treatment

by Laren Bays &

Robert Freeman-Longo

SaferSocietyPress

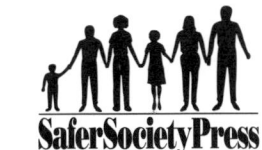

PO BOX 340 • BRANDON, VT 05733-0340

PHONE: (802) 247-3132

Copyright © 1989
Laren Bays & Robert E. Freeman-Longo
Sixth Printing, 1995
Seventh Printing, 1997

All rights reserved. No part of this publication may be reproduced, stored in a retrieval system, or transmitted in any form or by any means, electronic, mechanical, photocopying, recording, or otherwise without prior permission of the copyright owners, except for brief quotations included in a review of the book.

Design: Whitman Communications, Inc.

Editors: Euan Bear & Fay Honey Knopp

ISBN: 1-884444-25-3

Order from:

The Safer Society Press
PO Box 340
Brandon, VT 05733-0340
(802) 247-3132

$12.00
U.S. Funds only
Vermont residents, please add sales tax

Acknowledgments

The Safer Society Press appreciates the comments and suggestions of the sex offenders incarcerated in the Connecticut and Vermont state prison systems and of Rita MacDonald, director of the Vermont Treatment Program for Sexual Aggressors, all of whom read and critiqued this manuscript. We are grateful for the shared perspective of the child abuser in a Vermont prison that appears in the front of the workbook.

Letter from a Child Abuser
Who Read This Workbook

EARLY IN MY TREATMENT MY THERAPIST SAID TO ME, "Your task in therapy is to change your entire style of being alive." I was stunned. I didn't understand what she meant. I felt frightened, overwhelmed by the enormity of it. "I'm a sex offender," I thought. "I'm in jail because I need to change my deviant sexual behavior. Why is she dragging in the rest of my life?"

As I progressed in treatment, I came to understand what she meant. My deviant and destructive cycles are not separated from the rest of my life. They have been a part of all aspects of my life, and making the changes I needed to make would indeed change my entire style of being alive. I learned how out-of-touch with my feelings I had been. I discovered how distorted much of my thinking was. I examined my attitudes and their effects on my behaviors. And I began to see how they were all linked together and how my deviant cycle worked.

It was only after I knew my deviant cycle and could recognize the cues which tell me I am in it that I could develop techniques to intervene and break it. This workbook is designed to help you understand your cycles and how they operate in your life. You won't do this in a day ... or a week ... or a month. You will be working to change patterns of behavior you have built up and practiced for years, and it will take time, and patience, and diligence. To do it you must be honest, brutally honest, with yourself and with those whom you trust. You will have to admit things about yourself that you have never admitted before. It is difficult, painful work. I found it the most difficult work I have ever done. And the most rewarding! I have control over myself that I never had before. I know that by using the tools I have created for myself, I can live the rest of my life without abusing anyone else. I find I have the ability to create relationships deeper and more meaningful than any I've ever had before. I am real ... I work hard to avoid role-playing and attempting to be what I think others want me to be. I am honest. And for the first time in my life, I feel good about who I am. I like me.

I am now beginning the process of reintegrating into the community. As I do that, I recognize that my journey to self-knowledge continues. The hard work continues and it will for the rest of my life. So do the rewards. As you begin your journey, I wish you the best. I hope you find it as rewarding and exciting as I have. This workbook will provide you the structure and guidance you need to begin changing your behaviors. You must provide the determination and courage.

**A Child Abuser Treated in the
Vermont Treatment Program
for Sexual Aggressors**

Contents

5 Introduction

Part I - Links & Chains

7 Chapter One *Understanding Cycles*
What is a Cycle? / Why Study the Cycle? / Links in a Chain / Cycles Spinning on Cycles Spinning … / Assignments

17 Chapter Two *Perception: The Triggers in Your Environment*
Perceptions, Attitudes, and Behavior / Assignments

20 Chapter Three *Thinking Links*
Thinking Leads to Behavior / Thinking Links and Feelings Are Related / Assignments

27 Chapter Four *Feeling Links*
The Great Gamble / Links in the Chain / Assignments

33 Chapter Five *Values Clarification*
Making Choices / Hide and Seek / Assignments

38 Chapter Six *Links and Chains That Maintain Your Cycle*
Links / Links Create a Chain / Behavior Chains Link Into a Cycle / Assignments

Part II - The Cycle

50 Chapter Seven *Your Deviant cycle: Putting It All Together*
Phases of the Cycle / A Cycle Goes Around / Assignments

58 Chapter Eight *Setting Yourself Up: The Justification Phase*
Thinking Defects / Assignments

63 Chapter Nine *The Secrets of the Cycle*
Assignments

72 Chapter Ten *Interrupting Your Cycle: Basic Interventions*
Specific Intervention Techniques / General Interventions / Assignments

78 Recommended Readings

Introduction

CONGRATULATIONS AND THANK YOU for acquiring *Why Did I Do It Again? Understanding My Cycle of Problem Behaviors*. This guided self-help workbook is the second in the Sex Offenders' Studies (S.O.S.) Series that have been developed to help people who have problems with sexuality and aggression. We recommend that you read and complete the first workbook in the series, *Who Am I and Why Am I in Treatment?* before beginning this one. Each workbook builds on the information of the previous one. If you don't read the workbooks or chapters in order, you may feel confused, lost in the material, and discouraged.

In *Who Am I?* you read a brief overview about behavioral cycles and completed assignments that helped you identify some of your own cycles. This workbook covers similar cycles of behavior, but is more detailed and helps you learn more about yourself. After you have studied your cycles, you will discover they are the basis for almost everything you think, feel, and do. You can use this information in treatment to help you change your life for the better.

Understanding and exploring your cycles will take a lot of time and effort. To do it well you have to be willing to look closely at yourself and get feedback from others. You must ask for feedback from your therapists, friends, and group members about what they see in your attitudes, thinking, feeling, and behavior. Hardest of all, you must really listen when they give you feedback. Asking for and hearing what others say about you helps you learn to separate normal from destructive thoughts, feelings, and behaviors. By learning the differences you can learn how to detect your destructive cycles and how to stop them in your day-to-day life.

Each chapter in this workbook ends with homework assignments designed to help you better understand the material and practice what you have learned. If you do not understand an assignment, ask your therapist, group, or a close friend. Even if you do not understand a question completely, think about it, ask your group or a friend, and try your best to give good answers. We recommend that you not write in this workbook. Keep a separate notebook for writing each of your assignments. You should review your homework assignments with your therapist or group.

As in *Who Am I?*, we strongly recommend that you join a treatment program for sex offenders. However, in many places specialized treatment is not available. If you must work on your own, we recommend you share your assignments with a friend or someone else you can trust to give you accurate, honest feedback.

Again, we congratulate you on your efforts to help yourself through treatment. We sincerely wish you good fortune in your treatment program and in completing this workbook. If you are working on your own, we hope that this workbook will be a useful tool for you and that you will continue to work at making changes in your life. **GOOD LUCK!**

Laren Bays   Rob Freeman-Longo
Portland, Oregon   *Safer Society Foundation*

PART I LINKS AND CHAINS

1.
Understanding Cycles

What is a Cycle?

THE WORD CYCLE IS DERIVED FROM the word circle. In fact a cycle is like a rotating circle. A cycle refers to a pattern that repeats over and over. The cycle's pattern may be ways of feeling, thinking, behaving, or a combination of all of them that repeat in your life. You might think of it like the loop that a bicycle chain forms on a bike. Each time you pedal, the chain moves; as the chain moves, the bike goes forward. The bicycle chain goes around and around. It repeats the same pattern over and over. You drive the bicycle chain; the bike moves and you have to steer it or crash. If the bicycle chain were to break one link you could repair it; it would be a bit shorter but it would still work. But when you take several links out of the chain, it breaks down and will not operate.

Cycles of behavior are like a bicycle chain: they are made up of links that together form chains; the chains join to form the cycle, which repeats over and over, around and around. Ways of perceiving, thinking, feeling, and acting each make a link in the cycle. When put together they form a complex behavioral cycle that is acted out over and over. Like a bicycle chain, a deviant cycle can be broken, but only by breaking or removing many links.

Why Study the Cycle?

Why study cycles? Healthy or unhealthy cycles are the basis of your behavior and strongly affect your life. When you begin to learn about cycles, you will better understand yourself and your behaviors. By understanding how your behavior is produced, you will be better able to intervene and change destructive behaviors. Making positive changes means you are on the road to leading a life that is happier, more satisfying, and healthier.

This workbook is about cycles of behavior in general and your own in particular. As you work through it you will discover some cycles that assist you to live a balanced healthy life. You will also discover cycles that are unhealthy and lead you toward deviant and destructive behavior. When you understand the relationship between the start of a cycle and its end, you will have some of the knowledge and tools that help you avoid deviant behavior.

Your deviant cycle is a part of your overall "life cycle." Your life cycle is very complex. When it is healthy and productive, you are growing and not injuring yourself or others. At other times your life cycle may change to a "deviant," or less healthy cycle; your cycle "deviates"—it is different from normal. This deviation may be sexual or involve other areas of your life. It is possible to have deviant cycles of anger, gambling, or depression. When we use the term "deviant cycle" we mean a recurring pattern of behavior that makes you less effective, less healthy, or prone to inappropriate or criminal behavior.

At times your deviant cycle may become more intense and obvious, as when you begin to plan a sexual crime. At other times the deviant cycle is operating within you and you may not be aware of it. As you work through this book you will learn to recognize both kinds of cycles.

There are at least nine good reasons for you to study your cycles, especially your deviant cycle.

1. **You learn what led up to committing your crime.**

   To stop your deviant behavior you must answer the question, "How did I get into the state of mind to commit my crime?" or "How could I have done it?" Many offenders think, "I'm not that kind of person, so why did I do it?" Understanding your deviant cycle will explain, in part, how you can go from acting wisely, feeling good, being productive and social, to acting criminally. The path from normal behavior to criminal behavior is not hard to see when you become aware of the decisions you made and the actions you took.

   The path from health to deviance is not simple. Many small decisions, seemingly unrelated to the result, led up to the big decision of committing a deviant act or sex offense. When you study the cycle you will discover the long route you took to acting out your deviant or criminal behavior. When you understand the decisions that led to your deviant activity in the past, you will understand how you got into a deviant state of mind.

2. **By studying your cycle you learn that each of your actions has several causes and several effects.**

   Everything you do has a cause, something that happened before and directly influenced what came after. When you decide to masturbate, something happens before you make that decision. Perhaps you feel lonely, or see an attractive woman, or have a sexual fantasy, or just feel sexual. Something happened to set the stage for what comes next. At first it may be difficult to understand what caused you to behave in a certain way. As you learn about the deviant cycle you will discover that each thought, feeling, situation, behavior, or perception causes some effect or change in you or in your environment.

   An effect does not have to be big; it may be small and subtle. For example, waking up and becoming aware of how your mouth feels may have the effect of making you want to brush your teeth. Perceiving how your mouth feels is then one of the causes that leads to brushing your teeth. When you understand your cycle you will learn about the causes (the behaviors, thoughts, feelings, and circumstances) that lead to your deviant behaviors.

3. **You learn how you usually react to thoughts, feelings, and environments.**

   When you understand your deviant cycle you can predict where particular types of thinking, feeling, and acting may lead. The ability to see the effects of your reactions in your behavior will help you control your deviancy and is a necessity for healthy living. For example, after you have learned about the cycle you will be able to predict both the long-term and short-term effects of drinking alcohol. You will be able to say how you will feel if you drink, how you might act, and how others respond to you. Knowing about the effects of your behavior gives you an important tool for controlling your life.

4. **You learn that your behavior is affected by every place you go and everything you see.**

   Different environments—friends, work, even movies—influence whether you think, feel, and act in healthy or in deviant ways. Some environments, like a topless bar, may influence you to act sexually. Other environments, like prison, may influence you to watch every move you make. As you get better at predicting how a particular environment may affect your feelings, thoughts, and actions, you will be able to find environments that encourage you to lead a healthy life and avoid environments that lead to deviancy.

Learning about the cycle will help you to understand the complexity of the relationship between your feelings, thoughts, and behaviors and your environment. You may feel angry and be in an environment (like a classroom) that encourages you to stay in control; or you may feel angry and be in an environment (like a bar) that encourages you to "let it all out." As you better understand your cycle you will be able to identify environments where you will be at greater risk to reoffend. You will also learn about environments that may start your feelings and thoughts heading in a direction that can lead you to deviant behavior.

5. **By studying your cycle you learn how your feelings influence your behavior.**

Learning about your cycle will help you to discover how your feelings contribute to your behavior. Consider, for example, the feeling of "righteous anger": you feel that you have been wronged and have the right to be angry. Offenders often feel righteous anger; they use it as an excuse to violate a law or get even, and they end up in more trouble than when they started. Learning to recognize unhealthy feelings and where they may lead is part of learning about the cycle.

6. **You learn how your thoughts influence your behavior.**

Your thoughts about yourself and the world contribute to your health or deviance. Errors in how you think about the world and yourself usually occur long before any problem behavior happens. If you never thought about deviant sexual behavior then you would not act deviantly. Even in what appears to be an impulsive, spontaneous crime, thoughts set the stage for the behavior. Learning what kind of thinking leads to deviant behavior and what kind leads to healthy behavior is an essential step in understanding your cycle.

7. **You learn how your beliefs about the world and yourself influence how you act.**

Most adults have old beliefs or fixed ideas that they grew up with. Some are accurate and healthy, and some are destructive. An example of an unhealthy fixed belief might be "all women are untrustworthy," simply because they are women. You might have learned it in your childhood if you were sexually abused by a woman or if the men in your family taught you to believe it. This distortion of reality ("all women can't be trusted") influences you to act suspicious or hostile toward women; your hostile behavior then influences others to avoid you or be angry at you. Unhealthy fixed beliefs lead you into trouble. Understanding what your fixed beliefs are and how they have contributed to your deviant cycle enables you to change in a healthy way. For example, once you realize that one of your beliefs is "all women can't be trusted," you can change that belief. You can learn that some women (like some men) can't be trusted. You can also learn how to decide which ones you can trust and which ones you cannot.

8. **Understanding your cycle teaches you how what you do today influences what you do tomorrow and in the future.**

Understanding your cycle teaches you where you are going. If you have a habit of being angry today, you will probably be angry tomorrow unless you make a conscious effort to change. If you have a habit of resentment this year, you will likely be resentful next year also. If you have a habit of laziness today, you will be lazy tomorrow. When you look deeply into your cycles you see that how you acted in the past influenced your later behavior. In an unconscious and unhealthy way you have been in control of your life for most of your life. What you decided to do one day led you to the next day's decisions. You can change this so that you have a healthy power over your future. It all depends on what you do today, each day.

9. **Understanding your cycle will teach you when and how to stop your deviant behavior.**

Understanding your cycle is a step toward developing tools to break an out-of-control cycle. When you have learned what environments, thoughts, feelings, and behaviors lead to unhealthy or dangerous situations, you can intervene to stop them. Even when there hasn't been any direct problem with a feeling or thought, you may need to intervene so it does not lead to deviant behavior. Learning about your deviant cycle teaches you where you are heading and when you must intervene. For example, loneliness by itself is not unhealthy, but in your deviant cycle it is an early warning sign that you need to intervene and make decisions about how to handle that feeling. You may decide to go to an AA meeting or call up a friend instead of running your old pattern of trying to drink your loneliness away. Knowing when to intervene is one result of understanding your deviant cycle.

Links in a Chain

A *link* is a small distinct part of a chain that connects one part with another. Links are the *single thoughts, feelings,* or *actions* that make up your cycle. If the links were not present to connect one behavior with another you would not continue with an action. Think about your morning routine. You might get up, think about having a cup of coffee, and go make coffee. The *link* between getting up and drinking coffee is the *thought* of coffee. If you come home from work and feel lonely, you might call your womanfriend. The *feeling* of loneliness is the *link* between coming home and calling your womanfriend.

Each of these links is connected to another link. You *feel* bored, *think* about going driving, *get* into your car, *feel* pleasure, *think* about going to the movies, and *drive* away in that direction. Each *thought, feeling,* and *behavior* in this sequence links what came before with what comes after. They are connected like the links in a chain. One link is connected to the next link, is connected to the next link, is connected to ... When you break any link in the chain, the chain is broken. You break your deviant cycle by breaking one link at a time.

When you look closely at any sequence of behavior you notice that there are many small links. These links are essential to the behavior; the chain of behavior would not continue without them. The link may seem very unimportant, but the entire chain of behaviors would stop if that link were not there. If you did not think, "I'd better get the paper," you would not read the paper. Thinking is an essential link. Part of your morning routine would stop if you broke that link. If you did not feel you needed to brush your teeth, you would be less likely to brush them. If you broke several links in your morning routine, the entire morning routine would come to a stop.

The First Link: Perception

A *perception* is what you see, hear, touch, taste, or smell. In order to recognize something you must become aware of it, you must perceive it. Perceptions are the result of information your senses receive and your brain processes. If you smell something burning, that is a perception. Seeing a car coming at you is a perception. Your awareness of your environment is the result of perceptions. Perceptions by themselves are not good or bad. How you respond to a perception is what is important.

A *trigger* is something that starts a bullet moving. In the same sense a perception may trigger healthy or unhealthy thoughts or feelings. For example, seeing a picture of a naked child is a perception. When you respond to the picture sexually, that feeling is an unhealthy response to the perception. Because you have responded sexually to the photo, that photo is a trigger for your deviant sexual feelings. Seeing a woman hitchhiking is a perception. If you are a rapist, seeing the woman may be a trigger for thoughts of picking her up and raping her. Perceptions often trigger or start a series of thoughts or feelings.

The Second Link: Thought

Thought refers to all mental activity: ideas, notions, opinions, beliefs, impressions, judgments, etc. Generally, you think about what you are doing, different situations you encounter, past events, future happenings, or other ideas. The human thought process provides you with the capacity to reason, use logic, use common sense, put together ideas, and a variety of other processes.

Your mind is seldom empty of thoughts. Even when you are sleeping your mind is active. You have dreams even when you do not remember dreaming. In your daily life your mind is active in an ongoing mental dialogue so habitual, so usual, that you hardly notice it. To see how active your mind is, try sitting in a quiet place and counting your breaths. See if you can focus on the counting without thinking of anything else. You'll be amazed at how much is going on in your mind without your ever being aware of it.

Thoughts govern just about everything you do. You do not have to be aware of the thoughts for them to influence you. Whether you are aware of them or not, even the simplest, most natural, ordinary action requires thought. The thoughts, "I think I'll make some coffee," or "I think I'll take a shower" come before doing these things. If you never thought about coffee you would never make coffee. Thought is necessary for action. You may not be aware of simple thoughts occurring throughout the day before you do something because routine thoughts are often abbreviated, shortened into personal mental shorthand. "I think I'll make some coffee," might be shortened to "coffee." "I hate him for what he did," might be shortened to "hate."

Thoughts are always present. Usually a *perception* precedes a *thought* which is followed by *action*. For example, you look through a magazine and see a picture of a woman. First you *see* the picture of the woman and then you begin *thinking* about how sexy she looks. Thinking about sex encourages you to *decide* to masturbate and you *reach* for your fly. Your *perception* led to your *thoughts* which led to your *decision* to masturbate and to your *action* of reaching for your fly. Thoughts make links that connect perceptions and actions.

When you allow your thoughts to dwell on the idea of doing something, those thoughts prepare you to do it. Sex offenders have thoughts and fantasies about committing their crimes before they actually do them. As a sex offender, your thoughts about deviant sex link your perceptions and your behavior.

Deviant thoughts are often based on *prejudices*, old habitual ways of thinking. These prejudices may be subconscious, the result of the distorted ways you learned to feel safe and powerful as a child. Often people are prejudiced without even knowing it. They have a habit of seeing a person of another race, a different background or sexual orientation, the other gender, or someone with a handicap and thinking, "I don't like that ..." Because of these old thoughts, their minds are not clear enough to be open to new experiences. Learning to be aware of these deeply rooted and half-hidden thoughts is one step toward breaking the cycle of deviant thinking.

The Third Link: Feeling

A *feeling* is an emotion or an internal sensation. You have many feelings. Feelings often happen after perceptions or thoughts. Feelings are your internal reactions to things that are going on around you and within you. When you *see* a person (a *perception*) who has been hit by a car, you may *feel* panic. Later as you *remember* the incident (a *thought*), you may *feel* sad. There is always a connection between what you think and what you feel; either one may happen first, but it is closely followed by the other. When you *feel* sad, you may *think* your life is horrible. On the other hand, when you *think* your life is horrible you may *feel* sad. Your feelings affect your thoughts; your thoughts affect your feelings. Being aware of what you are feeling is an important step in changing your life. Once you know you feel depressed much of the time, you can make decisions that will take you out of depression. When you do not know how you feel, you cannot make healthy decisions.

It is important to understand the emotions that are a part of your cycle. You may feel any or all of the following emotions as part of your deviant cycle: sadness, joy, fear, anger, fatigue, depression, happiness, love, hate, confusion, emptiness, frustration, contentedness, pain, hurt, and loneliness. These feelings often make the connection between your thoughts and your behavior.

As a sex offender you probably block your feelings. You deny that you feel emotions like sorrow, fear, or pain. It becomes a habit for you to cut off feelings that might help you understand how others feel; this habit makes it easier for you to commit a crime. When your capacity for feeling compassion is lessened, you become less human and you respond to others as if they are less than human. When you cut off old, painful emotions like fear, terror, helplessness, and confusion, you cut off all emotions; you may not feel fear, but you probably don't feel joy either. As you write out your deviant cycle, try to notice when certain feelings start and stop.

The Fourth Link: Behavior

Behavior means action, what you do. How you *behave* is the result of how you *think* and *feel*. If you feel like masturbating and you think it is okay, then you will probably masturbate. On the other hand, people who never have positive thoughts or feelings about deviant sexual acts do not commit sexual crimes.

Initially, most of your behavior is a result of your conscious thoughts. When you have frequently repeated these behaviors, they become habits and take very little thought. Sometimes behaviors become ritualized and compulsive; you feel you have no control over them. As you learn more about your cycle you will learn that you can stop compulsive behavior by changing the thoughts and feelings that precede it.

Behavior is not only what you do at this moment, but also the outcome of what you have done in the past. For example, suppose that in the afternoon you make a choice to go to the park. An hour later you decide to stop and watch some children play. Soon you see a boy going into the restroom and you decide to follow him in. If you never went to the park and weren't around children, you wouldn't have the behavior of molesting a child. Your earlier decisions made it easier for you to follow the boy into the restroom. When you chose to be with children, that behavior brought you one step closer to the molesting behavior.

The Chain Gang

A behavioral *chain* is a series of *behaviors, thoughts,* and *feelings* that are connected and follow one after another. Like an iron chain, it is made up of small connected links. When you pull one end of an iron chain, eventually the other end moves. In the same way, when you affect the beginning of a chain of thoughts, feelings, and behaviors, the end of the chain is also affected.

Consider the chain of behaviors involved in smoking cigarettes. First you feel bored or tense. Then you think, "Do I have any cigarettes?" Next you might check your pockets and get the pack and matches out. Lastly, you open the cigarettes, remove one, put it into your mouth, light the match, hold it to the end of the cigarette, and inhale.

If you affect the beginning of the chain by not buying cigarettes, then you disrupt the rest of the chain. But breaking one link will not stop your smoking. When you break another link by saying to yourself, "I won't borrow any cigarettes," then you have disrupted the chain even more. When

Figure #1: A Behavior Chain

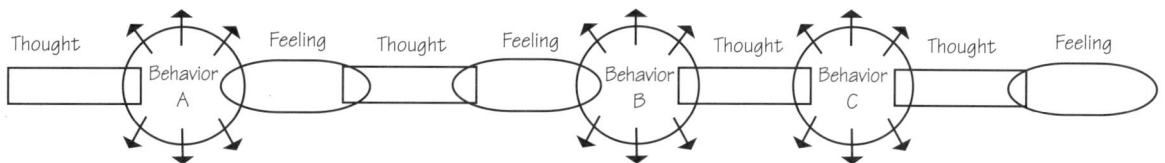

Links are connected to form a chain

you break a third link by leaving any area where someone is smoking, you break the chain even more. Break enough links and you stop smoking.

In a behavioral chain the thoughts, feelings, and behaviors automatically lead from one to the other. When drop-kicking a football, first you hold the ball (touch, a *perception*) and roll it in your hands so the laces are up (an *action/behavior*). You look down the field (sight, a *perception*), notice the left-side receiver isn't paying attention (a *perception* leading to a *thought*), feel strong, alert, and a little sly (all *feelings*), decide (*thought*) to kick it to him, raise the ball out in front of you (an *action/behavior*), and take two or three steps (another *action/behavior*). Finally, you decide (a *thought*) when and at what angle to drop the ball as you swing your foot forward to kick it (an *action/behavior*).

The first time you go through this chain of behaviors, it takes a lot of thought. At first you don't know what to do or how to do it. But after you have kicked enough footballs it takes only brief thoughts. Eventually the behavior becomes so automatic that once you start at the beginning, you move from one behavior to another without hesitation and with barely conscious thoughts. The more you have practiced a behavioral chain the more automatic it becomes. After a while if the chain starts it will go to the end with little awareness on your part. Everyone has many automatic chained behaviors. Think about the number of cigarettes that you have smoked or the miles you have driven without being aware of them.

A behavioral chain has a beginning and an end. You start your morning routine by waking up and automatically go through your morning until you end up going to work (the end of the chain). Once a chain of behaviors ends, it does not automatically repeat itself like a cycle does. Some examples of chained behaviors are washing your car, feeding your animals, cleaning your house, washing the dishes, etc. With these chains you don't automatically repeat the behavior over and over. You don't feed your dog just after you feed your dog. A chain may be a part of a larger cycle that does repeat.

Figure #2: A Broken Behavior Chain

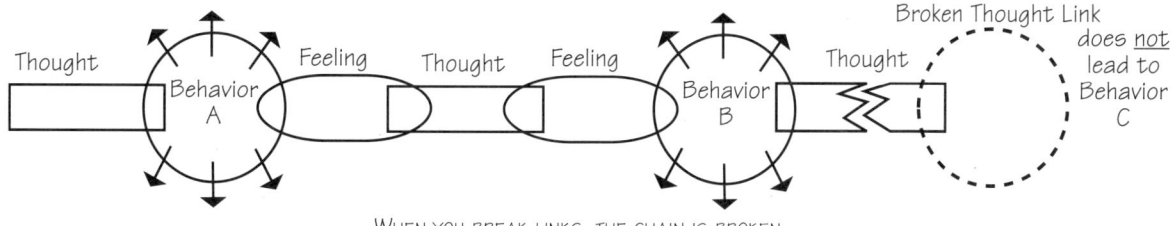

When you break links, the chain is broken

13

Cycles Spinning on Cycles Spinning ...

A cycle is a series of events that happens over and over. The cycle may be short or long, subtle or obvious. Your biological patterns are cycles of sleeping then waking, being hungry then eating, and finally going to sleep again, only to wake and start over. The links or chains you add on to this basic cycle make it complex and intricate.

You can have many different cycles each made up of several chains and links. The effects of your different cycles may be productive, as when you go to work or take care of your family. Or the effect may be destructive and end in behaviors like rape, child molesting, or addiction to drugs and alcohol. The work you do while going through this workbook will help you understand your cycles of behavior and enable you effectively to change deviant cycles into positive, healthy cycles.

Cycles make up your life and all that you do. You have learned about the parts of the cycle: *perceptions*, *thoughts*, *feelings*, and *actions* linked together in chains. What you *perceive* in your environment *triggers thoughts, feelings*, and *behavior*. These *links* connect to make the *chains* of your *cycle*. Each link is significant: even the smallest one can influence how you act, feel, and think.

Cycles are complex and you will learn more about them in the chapters that follow. Your deviant cycle also has *phases*, each containing its own small *cycles*, *chains*, and *links*. We have named these phases *Build-up, Acting-out, Justification,* and *Pretend-* (ing your life is) *normal*. The next four chapters deal with the links, chains, and cycles within the *Build-up* and *Acting-out* phases of your deviant cycle. When you work through all of the exercises in this book you will have a good understanding of how your deviant cycle works.

Chapter 1 Assignments

◎ **Do not write in this workbook** ◎

1a. List ten (10) reasons why it is important to learn about your deviant cycle. Nine are listed in this chapter; see if you can come up with a tenth. For each reason write what it means to you and explain how it can help you with your sexual deviancy problems.

1b. Give one (1) example from your life that shows how you could have acted differently if you had known about each reason listed above.

Hint: For example, suppose for Assignment #1a you put "understanding how feelings lead to deviant behavior" on your list of reasons. Then for Assignment #1b describe a time when that understanding would have helped you act differently. You might write, "If I had realized how feeling lonely led to my going into bars, I could have met a friend for coffee instead."

2a. Write down the first THOUGHTS that come to your mind when you read each of the following words:

| Police | Prison | Wife | Sex | Children |
| Rain | Beach | Lunch | Women | New York |

2b. Write down the first FEELINGS you have when you read the same list.

Hint: The purpose of this exercise is to help you see how one link (also known as a *stimulus*) immediately leads to another. This is how links are formed and a cycle begins.

3. Write down one (1) example from your life and one (1) example from someone else's life (two [2] examples for each word) for cycle, chain, and the different types of *links: feeling, perception, thought,* and *action/behavior*.

4. Think about what you read in the text. What is one way habits might form? Write down an example from your life of a habit that got formed this way. Be sure to write down the specific links that led to the habit.

5. Using words or a diagram, write down the details of three (3) different chains of behavior in your life. Be able to describe this process to your group or a friend if you are working alone.

Review these assignments with your therapist and with your group. If you are working on your own, share them with a friend or person you trust.

2.
Perceptions: The Triggers in Your Environment

PERCEPTION IS THE BASIS for much of what you do. It is the foundation of what you learn and what information you take in; it plays a significant role in shaping your behavior. Perceptions trigger your thoughts and feelings.

Of the five senses, vision and hearing are probably the two you rely on most for information about the world. Information you hear and see usually results in thoughts and emotions that lead to behavior. For example, when you see a couple walking together, you may think, "I don't have anybody special," and feel lonely. This thought and feeling might lead to an action: calling up a friend. Or you hear splashing and yelling from the river. You think about whether someone might have fallen in, feel excited, and take action by going to help. As you learn about the links that form behavioral chains, you will find that many of them begin with hearing or seeing something.

Perceptions, Attitudes, and Behavior

What you perceive through your senses affects your attitudes or beliefs about the world around you. If you grew up or now live in a violent environment, your attitudes about violence have been shaped by those perceptions. Perceptions affect attitudes, which affect behavior. Your attitudes and your behavior are like two sides of a coin. They are inseparable, and though they may look different, they are really the same. If your attitude about people who get loud and rowdy when they are drunk is that they are obnoxious, you probably do not spend much time around them. You may have developed these attitudes and behaviors in your childhood or they may have come from the people you are with and the places where you now spend time. Dennis got his bad attitude from his father.

> ### "Dumb" Dennis
> Dennis's father didn't like him very much. It seemed that no matter how hard Dennis tried to do things "right" (his father's way), nothing he did was ever good enough, or so his father told him over and over.
>
> When Dennis washed the car like he was told to, his father pointed out streaks on the finish or spots he missed. If there weren't any, his father made up some other reason the car wasn't washed right. When Dennis mowed the lawn, his father complained about the uneven lines or yelled at him for not cleaning the lawn mower correctly.
>
> Over and over Dennis heard from his father words like, "You're stupid." "Can't you learn to do anything right?" "You're always making mistakes." "Why bother?" "You'll never amount to anything." Sometimes his father even yelled, "I wish you were never born!" All Dennis heard was that he was dumb and good for nothing.

Dennis eventually learned to believe the things his father said about him. He began to question his abilities. His life became a "self-fulfilling prophecy" of failure. A self-fulfilling prophecy develops when you predict that you can't do something and then find out that you can't. You believe that the negative things people say about you are true, so you begin to act like they're true, and then they become true.

After years of listening to his father, Dennis believed he was stupid and couldn't do anything right. He gave up trying, acted stupid, and played dumb. He decided there was no use in trying since he would be picked on whether he did something right or not. As a result, Dennis's self-esteem, his idea of his own worth, was very low. He felt like he wasn't as good as other people.

Perceptions Affect Behavior

What led to Dennis's negative self-concept? Why did he give up? As a child, he perceived that his world was full of putdowns and failures. This led to a feeling that he was worthless. In turn Dennis's feelings set the foundation for his behavior. His perceptions triggered thoughts and feelings which became the links to his behavior.

The links in Dennis's chain of worthlessness may have formed like this:

Perceptions: You're stupid! You never do anything right!
Thoughts: He's right, I've screwed it up again.
Feelings: Why bother. It's hopeless.
Behavior: Gives up or never even starts.

Every day, when you take in information through one of your senses, a link begins to form. One link leads to another link which leads to still another link, etc.

The sights and sounds you fill your environment with strongly affect how you think and behave. Many people say that they have no control over their environment. But even if you are in a maximum security prison or a county jail, you still have a choice. You can spend your time and energy reading books or finding and being in environments where men work on changing themselves and speak positively about the future, as in treatment programs, school, or chapel. Or you can spend it in environments where men talk about future crimes, feed their hatred, and act violently. You have a choice.

What Could You Change?

As a young child, Dennis did not have control over his environment. He learned from what he perceived. As an adult you do have some degree of control over what you perceive. You can choose what you hear. You can find healthy friends. You can listen to music that helps you to feel uplifted. You can spend time in spiritual fellowship. You can choose what you see. You choose the books you read, the movies you watch, and the photos you look at. Stopping sexual deviancy means breaking the links that lead to criminal thinking. Doing it well means learning how to control what you perceive.

If you have raped, you will have to make yourself stop watching hitchhikers, women on the street, women in bars, women in the neighborhood. You will want to get pornography out of your life. You have to make sure that you do not get into situations where you are likely to see vulnerable women. One way of controlling your perceptions is for you to decide that you need a curfew so you do not walk in neighborhoods at night.

If you have molested children, you will want to control your perceptions by not being around children: no going to playgrounds, video arcades, shopping malls, or toy stores; no watching movies with children in them; no talking to children on the phone; no dating women with young children.

What you perceive starts a chain of thoughts, feelings, and behaviors. One important step toward controlling your deviant behavior is identifying the perceptions that influence you. By monitoring and controlling your environment so you do not intentionally encounter the sights and sounds linked to your abusive behavior, you will be on the way to freedom from sexual deviancy.

Chapter 2 Assignments

∞ Do not write in this workbook ∞

6a. Think back to when you were a child. What types of perceptions do you recall that triggered negative thoughts or feelings and the behaviors that followed? Give at least ten (10) examples.

Example:

PERCEPTION	FEELING or THOUGHT	BEHAVIOR
Saw Dad hit brother	Felt afraid	Hid in my room
Saw Dad drink and get angry	Confused thoughts	Left the house
Saw Mom cry a lot	Felt sad	Talked to her
Saw friend hurt by girl	Angry, confused	Avoided girls

6b. Now make a list of perceptions that triggered positive thoughts and feelings and subsequent behaviors. Give at least ten (10) examples.

Example:

PERCEPTION	FEELING or THOUGHT	BEHAVIOR
Heard Mom say "I love you"	Felt cared for	Relaxed
Saw brother get good grades	Felt proud	Did my homework
Heard Dad tell jokes	Funny thought	Laughed a lot

7. List ten (10) environments that are not healthy for you. List ten (10) things in the environment that may encourage you to engage in deviant behavior.

Review these assignments with your therapist and with your group. If you are working on your own, share the assignments with a friend or person you trust.

3. Thinking Links

NOW THAT YOU KNOW about how perceptions influence your thoughts and feelings, we will look at the thinking links that result from your perceptions. The feeling links will be covered in Chapter Four. Thinking links can be triggered and affected by your feelings and feelings can be affected and triggered by your thinking. The links to your behavior are continuously acting and interacting with each other.

Thinking Leads to Behavior

How you think determines how you act. When you are full of violent, angry thoughts you will act violent and angry. When your thoughts are very confused, you probably act confused. When you think one way over and over, you will act that way. With repetition that behavior will become a habit.

For example, if you think hitting your wife is the only way to feel in control, you start hitting your wife; eventually it becomes a habit. Once you have a habit, the habitual behavior does not require much thinking. The behavior has become automatic and unconscious, like tying your shoes. You don't have to think about each step of how to tie your shoes—you just do it.

While some behavior is habitual, much of it requires thought, especially if it is not repeated often or if it is different each time it occurs. For example, playing checkers requires thought. Even if you play checkers every day, each game is a little different and your opponent may be different. So you must think about each move. If you move just out of habit, you will lose.

Some deviant sexual behaviors are simple and repetitive—like cruising bars, aimless driving, looking at possible victims and masturbating—and become mindless habits requiring no conscious thought. You perform these behaviors over and over, almost like a ritual. You may use them often to help keep you in a state of mind that forgets the real world.

Many other deviant behaviors require a lot of thought. Your thinking might be in the form of planning, fantasizing, or self-talk (what you tell yourself in your mind about what is going on around you and how you feel). Your thinking is always flawed or distorted when you are in a deviant sexual cycle. No matter which type of thinking you are doing, if you are planning a crime you are not thinking clearly. To change your life you can't just change the bad behaviors; you must learn to change how you think. You need to understand your flaws in thinking to change your deviant behavior.

"Stinking Thinking" Leads to Deviant Behavior

No one likes to be told that their thoughts and feelings are flawed or distorted. But many people occasionally think, feel, and behave in distorted ways—like getting a flat tire and calling the car "stupid." Clear, effective thinking would be telling yourself that you need to check your tires routinely to make sure they are not getting bald or don't have nails in them.

When you look closely at your life, you find that your deviant cycle involves "thinking errors," lies you tell yourself, and other distortions. In this workbook we call this kind of "stinking thinking" a *thinking defect*. Two forensic psychologists, Drs. Yochelson and Samenow, have described a series of thought and behavior patterns used by criminals.[1] These thinking defects are very specific about what goes on in an individual's mind and can apply to anyone. Below is a list of some thinking defects (adapted from their list) sex offenders usually use. When you are honest with yourself, you will recognize a number of them in your own thinking.

1. **Playing Dumb:** No self-confidence, "I'm too dumb to do it right." "I can't keep up with him." Thoughts focus on giving up, not trying, or what's the use in making an effort, often leading to self-fulfilling prophecy (remember "Dumb" Dennis?). "I never do anything right so there is no point in even trying." Thoughts focus on worthlessness, low self-esteem, inadequacy, and helplessness. "Nobody likes me, everybody hates me." "I'm no good."

2. **Ranting and Raging:** Thoughts focus on anger, outrage, hostility, and revenge. Anger becomes the central theme that affects the rest of your thoughts. Example: "I'd like to kill that SOB." "They have no right to treat me this way, I'll make them pay for it." Raging like a wounded bull becomes a tool for manipulation; part of the time it is not even real.

3. **"The One-and-Only":** Thoughts focus on excessive pride, narcissism (total focus on yourself, being self-absorbed above all else), conceit, vanity, being self-centered. "If I want it, I'm smart enough to get it." "My needs always come first in this house." "That therapist is dumb, he can never understand me." "I'm tough, I can do whatever I want." Thoughts focus on seeing yourself as unique, atypical, different, special, and above others. "I'm different, those rules don't apply to me."

4. **The Dominator:** Thoughts focus on control, overpowering others, demanding from others, commanding others to do what you want. "Those guys are so dumb, I can talk them into anything." "She'd *better* do what I want."

5. **Polarizing:** Thoughts focus on seeing the world as two clearly different sides. Things are polarized, either one way (like at the North Pole) or another (like at the South Pole). What you think about is either right or wrong with no gray area in between. "All women are out to get what they can from men." "You can't trust a woman." "Homosexuals are dirt." "Everybody I'm friends with in prison is innocent."

6. **Scatterbrained:** Unable to stay on track in a conversation. Your thinking is confused, involving a series of scattered and fragmented pieces, usually to cover up, distract attention from, or avoid unpleasant situations.

7. **Great Expectations:** Unrealistic optimism to the point of absurdity, grandiose ideas of what is possible and what will happen. "I can plan the perfect crime." "The cops will never get me." "I'll make a million on this deal."

8. **Trash City:** Everything is bad, can't see potential good or anything positive in people, events, situations, etc. "No one can be trusted to do things right." "What's the use, they'll screw it up again this time."

9. **Lies, Secrets, and Silence:** Dishonesty, big lies and little ones, including avoiding the truth. "I really wasn't in her room, I only walked by it." "I only talked to the woman, I never touched her." "I've never done anything like this before."

10. **Paranoia:** Constant suspicion, thinking that others are out to get you, ridicule you, or put you down. "If I show my feelings they will make fun of me." "I think they are trying to set me up." "They're talking about me behind my back." Thoughts focus on not trusting people or situa-

---

[1] See Yochelson, S. & Samenow, S.E. (1977). *The Criminal Personality*, Vols. I & II. Dunmore, PA: Jason Anonson, Inc.

tions. "The government never does what it says." "You can't trust a cop." "My womanfriend will go out with anyone when I'm not looking."

11. **One-track Mind:** Thoughts narrow down to one idea, one track, or one side of an issue, blocking out everything else. Locking onto a specific thought and being inflexible. Closed to suggestions or other ideas. "My way is the only way."

12. **Projecting:** Taking your own problems or ways of dealing and putting them on others. For example, someone who lies all the time might think: "I can't believe what they tell me, because people lie all the time." "If it's true of me, it's true of you."

13. **The Victim:** Victimized thinking, focusing on seeing the world as an unjust, unfair place. You turn events around in order to show yourself as the victim, the target, the underdog. "The judge was really unfair in giving me all maximums and running my sentences consecutive; after all, the victim wasn't hurt that bad."

14. **Mean-and-Nasty:** Thoughts focus on being belligerent, hostile, aggressive, rude. "I'll screw them but good, who do they think they are telling me what to do."

15. **"Not My Fault":** Irresponsible thinking. You avoid taking any personal responsibility for your life or anything that happens in it. "She did it." "It's not my fault that we don't have any money." "It's not my fault that I had a car wreck." "I don't give a damn who did it, it wasn't me."

16. **Denial:** Pretending things aren't as bad as they are, denying the truth, often to yourself as well as to others. Avoiding being honest, open, and truthful. "My problems will go away if I don't think about them." "Hey, I like to drink a little, I don't really have a problem with it." "I've got the flu, not a hangover." "I didn't do anything wrong."

17. **Blaming:** Pushing your responsibility off on someone else, not being accountable for your acts. "The kid wanted sex, he came on to me."
"She wanted to have sex, then later called it rape." "He wants to keep our room clean so it is his responsibility, I have nothing to do with it." "The alcohol was just there, I didn't go and get it."

18. **"All Mine":** A false sense of ownership, a feeling of being entitled. "I need this more than they do, so I'll borrow it." "It's my right, I am entitled to it." "I paid for dinner, she owes me sex." "They're my kids, I can do anything I want with them." "Possession is nine-tenths of the law."

19. **Worrywart:** Anxiety, focusing on fear, dread, distress. "If I talk about that I'll lose everything." "I'm going to die a violent death anyway." "I'll never make it in prison."

20. **Clinging Vine:** Can't do anything by yourself, relying on others for things you could do for yourself. Being over-dependent. "I can't go on living without her—who'll do my laundry and cook my dinner?" "I'll never make it if you leave me." "I can't go through this by myself."

21. **Phony Fawning:** Being superficial, insincere, running a con to get what you want. "If I make up a good excuse, she won't be angry."

22. **"Later, Man":** Procrastinating, avoiding responsibility by putting things off, being lazy. "I'll clean the kitchen later, I want to watch the football game now." "I'll pay the rent next week, it's only a few days late."

23. **"Who Cares":** Indifference, apathy, detachment. "Who cares what they think." "It doesn't matter if I'm rude or not." "So what, it won't affect me."

24. **Doormat:** Being passive and unassertive. Giving in, going along with others' plans. Appeasing others even though you really don't want to. When you find a sneaky way to wreck the plans or get back at the people, it's called passive-aggressive. "I don't want to go out tonight, but if I say so then she will be angry." "I don't want them to smoke here, but I'm scared they won't like me any more if I say anything." "I am

afraid to say no when people ask me to do things I don't want to."

25. **"Not So Bad"**: Minimizing, belittling the significance of your behavior and its impact on others or on yourself. Trying to make events smaller, or reducing their importance. "I didn't really hurt the child, I was just teaching her about sex." "She'll get over it, I didn't rape her that bad."

These are just some of the thinking defects. They become thinking habits after you use them long enough. Can you name additional thinking defects that you see in others or yourself? These defects can act as *thinking links* in a behavior chain that forms a cycle of destructive behavior.

Fearful Frank

Frank never feels comfortable around people his own age. He would like to be with adults, but thinks to himself, "I'm worthless, no one would want me as a friend." He is insecure, and acts withdrawn and quiet. Frank feels he can't talk with people and is fearful of meeting new friends. He usually feels depressed when he is around adults. Frank is afraid that someone will make fun of him or play jokes on him that will make him look stupid. When he sees someone talking, he automatically thinks they are talking about him. Because of his behavior—acting withdrawn, quiet, and defensive—adults feel suspicious of him, think he is strange, and avoid him.

To protect himself from their suspicion, Frank lies to them. The lies get him into big trouble. Then Frank gets more depressed and starts drinking. While drunk, Frank convinces himself that adults hate him and are out to get him. Then he thinks, "Children aren't like adults. They aren't bad. Children are loving, open and accepting." Before long, Frank starts fantasizing about how nice it is to be with children. As a result, Frank turns to children to meet his needs for love, affection, power, and control. Before long he finds a victim.

As you can see from Frank's story, several defects in thinking led him to molest a child. The first defect was *Playing Dumb*. Frank told himself that he was worthless and inadequate and that everyone really hated him. Because of this distorted thinking Frank isolated himself. When Frank stopped talking with people, stopped attempting to make friends, others stopped trying to talk to him. When they stopped trying to be friends with him, Frank thought, "No one cares about me." It confirmed his sense of worthlessness.

Extreme suspicion and projecting led to Frank's second thinking defect, *Paranoia*. Frank knew that he lied to lots of people, and he expected that people would not like him because of it. He also expected that they lied to him (another thinking defect—can you name it?). So when he saw others talking, he assumed that they would react like he would, that they were talking about ways to get even with him. This distorted thinking, triggered by Frank's observations, led to paranoid behavior: further withdrawal from others and lying.

Frank's next thinking error was the *Lies, Secrets, and Silence* defect. He started to lie. The more he lied, the more other adults thought he couldn't be trusted and the more they avoided him. When he approached people, they would tell him anything so they could get away. He knew that what they said was just an excuse not to spend time with him.

The fourth thinking defect was *Polarizing*. Frank's fear of adults led him to think unrealistically about the difficulty of being friends with adults. His concrete, polarized, no in-betweens thinking made it easy for Frank to see children as good and trustworthy and adults as bad and untrustworthy. All these negative feelings and thinking defects led to Frank's deviant fantasies about children as sexual partners, resulting in his moving toward the Acting-out phase of his deviant cycle by setting up situations where he could molest children. He has been acting out his deviant cycle since he was a teenager.

Thinking Links and Feelings Are Related

Thoughts seldom occur without accompanying feelings, nor do feelings happen without thoughts. You have fairly consistent patterns of thinking and feeling. Even in completely different situations, these thought and feeling patterns remain stable. As you get older and practice them they become more fixed; eventually they become habits.

Frank's story shows how his habits of thinking and feeling worked together to form a destructive cycle. Once a destructive cycle has started, many of the thoughts and feelings are not the result of what is really going on in the world. Instead they are the result of habit and may have nothing to do with reality. So you may have a thought, "He hates me." This gives rise to feelings of fear, distrust, and hatred. You begin to act on these feelings. The other person now becomes aware of your feelings and in turn feels fear, distrust, and hatred. We create our own reality in just this way. By his attitude and behavior, Frank created suspicion and rejection.

There are other ways that sex offenders create their own reality. One way is by thinking they cannot trust others, especially authority figures. When they begin to think in this *polarized*, no in-betweens way about ALL people, it results in feelings of anger, resentment, and fear. In their minds they begin to live in a terrible world.

The first step in changing distorted thinking patterns is to identify your thinking patterns and defects. Next identify the feelings you experience while your thinking defects are present. Look for the connections between the way you think and feel. Once you begin to identify these thoughts and feelings, you can look at them objectively and come to realize how they influence you toward deviant behavior.

You will probably find several common patterns of thoughts and feelings operating in your life. For example, when you are uncomfortable with meeting people, consider what you think just before seeing them. Perhaps you think they will not like you or they are stuck up. These thoughts then lead you to feel guarded and suspicious when you meet them.

The second step is to counter your distorted thoughts with reason and reality. When you think you are basically a nice guy, you might look at your history and think about how many people you have hurt during your life. It might open your eyes about how destructive you really have been. On the other side, when you think you are worthless, you might consider what you could achieve and who you could help if you worked at it for the next five or ten years.

The third step is to replace your thinking defects with realistic thoughts. When your thinking comes from the *Paranoia* defect (the world is out to get you), try replacing this thought with one that says you can find people you can trust. When you are *Playing Dumb*, thinking that you are not capable of accomplishing anything, consider how complicated your crime may have been. If you could do that, you can also do something more positive.

The last and hardest step is to practice what you have learned. Habits are hard to break. Putting your new thoughts into practice often so they become your usual thoughts takes time and effort. You can learn and practice several techniques to help in this process using our next workbook *How Can I Stop? Breaking My Deviant Cycle*, S.O.S. Series – Number Three.

In summary, *thinking defects* are the result of habit. They are *triggered* by what you *perceive* and lead to *deviant feelings* and *behaviors*.

Chapter 3 Assignments

∞ Do not write in this workbook ∞

8. Write down at least ten (10) thinking defects that apply to you. Give an example of how you have used each defect in your life. Use the list of thinking defects in this chapter and other thinking defects you may have discovered.

    Example:
    "Later, Man": I put things off, like paying my bills, which causes me problems. I am usually late. It has affected me in that everyone thinks I'm unreliable.

9. List at least five (5) examples of how your thinking defects (thinking links) led to behaviors that were involved in your sexual offense(s).

    Example:
    I would tell myself, "No one cares about me" and isolate myself.
    I would think, "What's the use?" and use drugs.

10. Review the list from Assignment #8. List at least one rational argument that explains why the thinking defect was unreasonable. Be sure to include a reasonable alternative for each of the ten thinking defects you used.

11. Write out a deviant cycle, using ONLY your *thoughts* and your *reactions* to them, showing how you got into the mind-state of committing your crime. Your assignment should look something like this example, except you fill in the thoughts and reactions in your own words.

    Example:
    BUILD-UP phase: Thinking ——> Reaction ——> Thinking ——> Reaction ...
    peaking in the ACTING-OUT phase: Thinking ——> Reaction ... through the JUSTIFICATION phase and back into the PRETEND-NORMAL phase.

    Hint: Don't worry if you don't yet understand what the JUSTIFICATION and PRETEND-NORMAL phases are about. Consider the names of these two phases, and think about what kinds of thoughts and reactions you might have during these parts of the cycle. If you're not sure, write your thoughts and reactions for these two phases in pencil; when we discuss them in more detail later, you can go back and fill them in more definitely.

12. Now make a second copy of Assignment #11 but leave LOTS of room since you'll be adding many more details to it! This will be the foundation for your full deviant cycle.

Review these assignments with your therapist and with your group. If you are working on your own, share the assignments with a friend or person you trust.

4.
Feeling Links

FEELINGS ARE PART OF YOUR EVERYDAY LIFE. Sometimes they are realistic and honest and sometimes they are distorted and blind. All of these feelings start with *perceptions* and *thoughts*. *Feelings* make up the third type of link that builds a *chain* of behavior. Often, thoughts and feelings occur together: sometimes a thought is connected to a feeling, and sometimes a feeling is connected to a thought. Your behavior is based on your thoughts and feelings and how they work together.

The Great Gamble

Like most sex offenders you are probably afraid of some of your feelings. You probably don't deal with them well or you try to avoid dealing with them at all. But there are three emotions you are probably very familiar with as a sex offender: depression, fear, and anger. All of your other feelings get covered over or hidden by these three emotions. The depression is usually the result of the mess your life is in. The fear is usually of losing control and being emotionally hurt. The anger is often a feeling of righteous anger: when things don't go the way you want them to, you feel the right to get angry about them. This kind of anger often makes you, the offender, feel like a victim, not in control of your life and feelings. Since your life as a sex offender is out of control, you often get angry because you feel controlled by others.

Depression, anger, and fear form a shield, a protective barrier that insulates you from feeling other emotions. With years of practice in your past, depression, anger, and fear become habits; other emotions seem unfamiliar and scary. Feelings like love, affection, patience, and peace are unfamiliar. When you do feel them, even a little, you feel vulnerable and out of control.

Being Vulnerable

Trusting others requires being vulnerable. Being vulnerable means that you put yourself in a position of being receptive and possibly of being hurt in the process. Sometimes trust hurts; it's scary, but it won't kill you. Relating to people in ordinary, everyday life involves levels of trust and vulnerability. When you buy something at a store, you are trusting that the store is not ripping you off. You trust that the quality of the merchandise matches your expectations (based on your examination, the company's reputation, and the cost). When you go out on a boat you are vulnerable to the ocean and the weather, and you trust the skill of the captain. Life requires you to be somewhat vulnerable, to trust others.

Love, intimacy, respect, friendship, and companionship all can come out of being trustworthy and trusting in a relationship. So trusting and being vulnerable can lead to great rewards! In any relationship, you have to decide whether the goal is worth the risk of being taken advantage of. Every time you trust someone you can grow in intimacy or you can be hurt. The ideal relationship is one where mutual trust works for both partners, allowing each person a sense of power and responsibility. When you marry or make a serious commitment to a relationship, you must learn to share trust and vulnerability with your partner. When only one partner is trusting and the other is not, the relationship doesn't work. Like many sex offenders, you may have grown up in environments where trust was used against you, or you were so untrustworthy that you projected those feelings and never trusted anyone else. When you never trust anyone your life is narrow and your options are limited.

If you never learned about knowing who to trust or how to choose trustworthy people, it can be scary to start. One way that many men try to keep from being scared and hurt is by not talking and not feeling, being "the strong, silent type." This kind of man keeps all his emotions squashed up inside. He doesn't flinch at anger or pain. He is often so rigid and over-controlled that when other strong emotions inevitably come, he cracks because he doesn't know how to deal with them.

You are probably pretty good at stopping your feelings and responding in only one or two ways. But there are many emotions that you can feel. Below is a partial list of feelings (Figure #3). Check yourself and see which ones you are familiar with.

When you first let yourself feel emotions you're not used to, you may feel out of control. You may think you are going a little crazy. This feeling soon passes as you get familiar with these new emotions. When you go one step further and share your feelings, you are taking a risk that others will be supportive, or that they'll make fun of you and put you down. You may feel vulnerable to another's potential to attack you.

Maybe you have experienced sharing your feelings with someone who made fun of you and put you down. If it happened to you several times, you probably learned to hide your feelings so you were not open to attack. This is not an excuse. The real key is learning how to choose people that you can trust. If you have had bad experiences in the past, it means that you need to look at and probably change how you choose friends.

No one likes to be put down, made fun of, or taken advantage of. While the fear is genuine, in most cases it is unrealistic. Unless you have chosen friends who regularly lie, cheat, and steal,

Figure #3: A List of Feelings

excited	hopeful	relieved	pleased	cheerful
amused	courageous	content	good	proud
friendly	loving	grieving	flattered	exhausted
sad	lonely	stupid	pained	discontent
regretful	aggravated	weary	ugly	ridiculous
hopeless	afraid	angry	beautiful	cautious
cowardly	satisfied	humble	modest	hateful
resentful	threatened	revengeful	jealous	envying
selfish	guilty	sensual	bad	mad
wary	up-tight	putdown	nervous	shaky
strange	detached	hostile	dreary	faithful
unique	happy	sick	judged	childish
humiliated	impatient	responsible	sorry	hungry
nauseated	thankful	obedient	wicked	smothered
joyful	smug	frustrated	paranoid	optimistic
surprised	ashamed	curious	anxious	determined
embarrassed	shy	pessimistic	bashful	miserable
indifferent	small	put-out	inadequate	insecure
perplexed	pensive	sympathetic	disgusted	hysterical
playful	ecstatic	open	fearful	energetic
depressed				

most people do not take advantage of your situation or feelings. But feeling that way is a habit that reinforces your fear. You probably try to protect yourself by covering up your feelings. You become emotionally insulated and socially isolated as a result.

Losing Control

You probably think that blocking your feelings means you are in control. Outwardly you may seem strong, but inside you are not in control at all—you are scared, anxious, and angry. These inner feelings affect you and how you relate to the world around you. You are not free to act flexibly and respond to the changing circumstances of life. Instead you become rigid and inflexible. In dealing with life and feelings, the object is to be like a tree: when the tree is flexible, it can bend with the wind; when it is too rigid, it will be blown over in a storm.

Not being able to act flexibly is being out of control. When you cannot respond to the changes of life except with depression, anger, and fear, you are out of control. When you are unable to choose how you will act and feel, you are being controlled by your defenses against others instead of acting for yourself. It is like a child who knows how to say "no" but is unable to say "yes." When you try to control yourself through depression, fear, or anger, you are actually out of control because these emotions are controlling you. When you are in control, you can feel appropriate emotions and respond to life flexibly.

Old Tapes

Music tapes are patterns of sound inscribed on strips of plastic so they can be played over and over again. They produce the same sounds regardless of what's going on outside the tape player. People have *tapes*, too, patterns of thinking, feeling, and reacting that get repeated over and over. Even when Sam was an adult and able to take care of himself, he reacted to people with his childhood "fear and anger" tapes. This old tape ran his adult life. Sam told himself, "No one is ever going to hurt me." When asked why he was cold and withdrawn, he said, "You can't trust anyone."

Like Sam, you probably carry *old tapes* of thinking, feeling, and acting that you play over and over. In a sense you have a prepared tape of emotional reactions. Every time you need to respond you play the same tape. After a while you may get sick of the same sounds, but until you make several new tapes you don't have much choice in how you act.

You may have several *old tapes* that control how you respond to various situations, people, or events. You may tell yourself, "People can't be trusted" or "People will take anything they can get." These old tapes can be erased once you decide to change the way you want to lead your life. Your feelings and thoughts about life and the world around you can be relearned. When you consistently change the way you think and feel, your behavior begins to change.

Silent Sam

Sam was raised in an abusive family. His parents expressed their anger and frustration at life by beating him. When Sam cried he was told to shut up and stop crying or he would be "given something to cry about." As a result, Sam learned to stuff his feelings. When he was beaten he tried not to cry or show any signs of hurt. Sam was afraid of his parents and angry about the way they treated him. But he learned that by covering up his feelings he wasn't so vulnerable and he avoided more beatings. Sam became silent and withdrawn from everybody. He felt protected and in control of the situation. When he left home as a young adult, Sam took his fear and anger with him. He did not make friends because he couldn't trust anyone, he was too afraid of what might happen. Sam learned to hide his true self and his feelings from everyone. He felt paralyzed around people.

Links in the Chain

In Chapter Three you learned that thoughts are linked to feelings and behavior. Feelings are another link to behavior. When you feel angry, you act angry. When you feel depressed and sluggish, you take a nap. *What you decide to do with your feelings makes the difference between healthy behavior and deviant behavior.* The behavior that comes from feelings does not have to be negative. For instance, when you feel bored you may begin looking for something to do. You may decide to paint or build a model airplane. With learning you can link a feeling to positive behavior: anger can be linked to splitting wood, working out with weights, or some other physical exertion. Fear can be linked to careful planning, boredom to creativity and new adventures. The key to making healthy emotional links is to be able to respond flexibly to your emotions.

Some feelings are pleasant, others unpleasant; some are neutral, and others might be good or bad depending on the situation. The two most important things to do with feelings are to experience and to talk about them. Jealous Jack gave up his freedom because he couldn't talk about his feelings.

Feelings and Thoughts Are Related

As you can see from this story, Jack's thoughts and feelings were related. He felt worthless and thought Pam was getting interested in another (better) man. Jack built up his suspicion until he just "knew" Pam was using him. He felt angry. In his mind he "knew" he wasn't good enough, was inadequate. Without even asking her, he "knew" Pam thought so too. He decided Pam was going to leave him and he feared being rejected. Jack's thoughts led to feelings that hurt Pam and made him feel bad.

But all those thoughts and feelings were just in Jack's head; they had nothing to do with anything that was really going on. He projected *his* feeling of worthlessness onto Pam and then got angry at her (while twisting things around so he was the "victim") for an action he believed she might take based on his faulty interpretation of

Jealous Jack

Since Jack was a child, he has been stuffing his feelings. Now Jack is 27 years old and serving his second prison sentence for rape. Jack met Pam after getting out of prison the first time. Jack was always afraid of expressing his feelings to others. He tried to act tough and independent with his friends. He played the same old tape in his relationship with Pam. He never let her know that things bothered him or that he felt weak and inadequate sometimes.

Pam got a job as a secretary. Every day she was surrounded by male co-workers. Jack became jealous about Pam talking and interacting with these men all day. He felt insecure and thought maybe he couldn't offer her the kind of life that other men could. Jack thought he wasn't good enough for her. He started to worry that Pam would become interested in another guy; he was afraid she might leave him. He began to feel angry as he thought about Pam leaving and he let his anger build. One day, Jack came home and blew up. He accused Pam of using him until she met another guy. No matter how hard she tried to tell Jack that she loved him, Jack would not listen.

Jack was afraid to tell Pam that he felt insecure and feared she would leave him. He could not admit that at times he just felt worthless. He was afraid of love and trust. When Jack felt scared, he got angry; when he got angry, he became defensive. When he was defensive, Jack used his anger to attack people instead of sharing how he truly felt. His emotions controlled him. He thought Pam was going to leave him and he feared her rejection. Jack began to push Pam away emotionally in argument after argument.

After Jack had the latest of many arguments with Pam, he left the house and went out drinking. While drinking he ran the same old tapes about how "women just use men." Jack began to feel depressed and full of rage. He left the bar and committed the rape that put him back in prison for the second time.

thoughts she wasn't even having. In reality, Jack's feelings (and the thoughts they were based on) were distorted. He didn't know they were distorted because he was afraid to talk about them.

Thoughts and feelings are a significant part of your chains and cycles. When your thoughts are distorted, they lead to confused feelings. The diagram below shows how Jack's feelings, thoughts, and behavior were connected.

An Emotional Safety Valve

Like most sex offenders, you probably hide your feelings of low self-worth, anger, and depression and let them build up until they come out in an explosion, a sexual crime. Stuffing your feelings is like creating an emotional pressure cooker.

A pressure cooker works by keeping heat and steam sealed in a pot. As the water inside gets hot, it turns to steam and builds up pressure. If the pressure just keeps building up, the pressure cooker explodes, burning anybody nearby. To prevent an explosion, pressure cookers have a safety valve built in to let off steam and relieve excess pressure.

Your feelings and emotions are just like the steam in a pressure cooker. They need to be acknowledged and expressed. When you express your feelings appropriately, you are creating a safety valve for yourself, releasing them a little at a time. The pressure doesn't build and your feelings don't explode and hurt anyone. There are many ways to express your feelings so they don't hurt anyone. You might talk with a friend or therapist, write your feelings down, cry, let yourself feel sad, or do something about the problem that is creating the feelings. Any of these releases requires you to be willing to trust and be vulnerable with someone. Dealing with your feelings serves as a release. Holding back your feelings creates pressure.

When you stuff your emotions, sooner or later the lid on your emotional pressure cooker blows off. A rapist who stuffs his anger and allows it to build up may finally explode and commit a rape. The child molester who does nothing about his feelings of inadequacy and insecurity starts to feel bad and turns to a child for comfort and later sexually abuses him or her.

It won't be easy dealing with new emotions. Not only are they scary for you, but other people are often scared of their own emotions as well as yours. They might act like they'd rather you kept your feelings inside. The key is learning to choose friends who aren't so scared of feelings and to share your feelings at appropriate times, in safe places, with people you can trust.

In summary, your *feelings* are *links* in a *chain* of *behaviors* and *cycles*. Feelings cannot be isolated from the way you think or act. To better understand your deviant cycle, you have to have an understanding of how *perceptions*, *thoughts*, *feelings*, and *behavior* are related.

Figure #4: FEELINGS, THOUGHTS, & BEHAVIORS

(Thought) "I'm not good enough" ——> (Feeling) hurt, anger, rejected ——> (Behavior) argument, blows up, leaves house ——> (Thought) "women just use men" ——> (Feeling) depression, rage ——> (Behavior) rape.

Chapter 4 Assignments

◈ Do not write in this workbook ◈

13. Using the list of feelings in Figure #3, write down the ones you usually feel. Next to each of the feelings, write down what you are most likely doing (behavior) when you feel that particular feeling.

    Example:
    1. HAPPY: Listen to music, sing, talk with friends.
    2. SAD: Cry, talk to my parents on the phone, sleep.
    3. FEARFUL: Withdraw from others, worry, avoid my problems.
    4. ENERGETIC: Jog, go for a walk, exercise, lift weights.
    5. DEPRESSED: Stay alone, use drugs and alcohol, skip meals.
    6. ANGRY: Get in fights, yell at people, drive fast, force sex.

14. Think back to the last sex crime you committed. Write down a detailed account of *how you felt* before, during, and right after your crime. In addition to your feelings, note what kinds of things you did as a result of your feelings, i.e., feeling bored and having rape fantasies, feeling excited about molesting a child and looking for a victim, feeling aroused and watching your victim and masturbating, etc.

15. Write out a deviant cycle that shows how you got into the mind-state of committing your crime using JUST your *feelings* and *reactions*. It should look something like this, except you fill in the names of feelings and what you thought or did as a reaction after having that feeling:

    BUILD-UP phase: feeling ——> reaction, feeling ——> reaction, feeling ——> reaction, climaxing in the ACTING-OUT phase, and then feeling ——> reaction through the JUSTIFICATION phase and back to the PRETEND-NORMAL phase.

    Hint: We will discuss the JUSTIFICATION and PRETEND-NORMAL phases later. For now, consider the meaning of the names of these two phases and think about what feelings and reactions you might have had. Write the feelings and reactions in your cycle in pencil and come back to it later when you have more information.

16. Now take the cycle of thoughts and reactions from Assignment #12 and add your feelings into it. Be sure to leave room since there is more of your cycle to come.

Review these assignments with your therapist and with your group. If you are working on your own, share the assignments with a friend or person you trust.

5.

Values Clarification

Your values are reflected in what you feel, think, and do. Values shape your behavior. They show what you think is important in your life. Your behavior expresses the values you hold. Unhealthy, unthinking, selfish behavior creates your deviant cycle, just as generous, kind, trustworthy, moral behavior creates healthy cycles. In order to understand your deviant cycle, it is important to see what good (positive, constructive) and bad (negative, destructive) values your behavior shows.

When you have criminal values, you act in criminal ways. When you hold healthy values, you act in healthy ways. How you act is closely related to what values, beliefs, and attitudes you hold. When you value your family, your behavior shows you working hard to support them. You support them emotionally by spending time with them and being kind and unselfish. You help them financially by providing food, shelter, and clothing. When you hold strong religious beliefs, you pray and try to be generous and forgiving. When you value your free time more than anything else, you probably act as though you resent spending time at work.

Making Choices

Choice, the process of making decisions, connects your values and your actions. You are constantly making choices. Every day you encounter many different situations where you are required to make some decision. Driving your car you must choose whether to stop for the yellow light or not. Feeling hungry you must choose what to eat, where to eat, and how much money to spend. Leaving work you must choose where to go. Feeling frustrated with your job you must choose between quitting or trying to adapt. You must always make choices in your life, even when the easiest choice is not to choose. By "not choosing" you make the choice that nothing matters; you just go along with whatever is happening.

Your values relate directly to your deviant cycle. When you are in the *Pretend-normal* phase of the cycle, your unhealthy values lead to choices that take you into the *Build-up* phase. When you are in the *Build-up* phase of the cycle your values lead to choices which take you into the *Acting-out* phase.

One way you will know when your values have changed is when you start making choices that take you *out* of the deviant cycle. For example, suppose that you value the excitement of having sex with a new woman more than you value intimacy with your wife. Reflecting that value, your behavior is to seek out new sex partners as part of your deviant cycle. However, suppose you enter treatment and your values change. You may decide you want to value a close relationship with your wife more than sex with other women. As your deviant values change, so does your deviant behavior.

The first place your unhealthy values show themselves is in the *Pretend-normal* phase. You are often a little bored, a little frustrated, or a little angry. The choices you make when you feel that way strengthen your healthy or unhealthy values. When you make choices based on your deviant values you start your deviant cycle. When you make choices based on your healthy values you start a healthy cycle.

Because your choices depend on your values it is important to find out what your values are. Ask yourself, "What is most important to me?" "What does success mean to me and how much do I value it?" "If success means money, do I value it enough to work at a job I don't like?" "Do I value job security so much that if a new more demanding job opened up I would not take it because I might fail?" "What values do I have about women and sexuality?" "How much do I value material possessions?" "How much do I value alcohol and drugs?" "What would I sacrifice to get drugs?" The answers you find to these kinds of questions may help you gain the keys to controlling your deviant behaviors.

When you hold unhealthy values you act in unhealthy ways. Earl found out how identifying his unhealthy values was a significant step toward his choosing a healthy life.

Hide and Seek

Values that are important to you are often hidden. They influence your choices without your awareness. Okay, so how do you discover your hidden values? You could just ask yourself, but then you might just say such wonderful stuff that no one could possibly understand why you're in treatment for sex offenses. The real key to discovering what your hidden values are is to *look at your behavior*. Your actions speak very loudly in showing what your true values are. For example, you may not want your wife to work outside the home, even though she may want to. In this case you are probably valuing your macho image of being "the great provider" and family boss, the tough guy who needs no help. You probably like the sense of control you feel over her more than you value her as an equal partner.

In the process of understanding your deviant cycle it is important to discover your hidden

Excitable Earl

Earl had a long history of sexual deviance. When he started therapy his therapist asked him to examine his value system. Earl discovered that his number-one value in life was, "If it's exciting, do it!" He put excitement at the head of his list of values. After some months in therapy Earl realized that he had sacrificed a lot of things for the momentary thrill of excitement. He left relationships saying, "She's too boring." He left jobs because it was "not interesting enough to stay here." He got into fights because "Saturday night is for excitement."

During therapy he began to see that he paid for his excitement by losing jobs, ending relationships, and wasting lots of money. Before Earl became aware of the high value he placed on excitement, this behavior seemed normal. Once Earl gained that awareness, he realized that he could decide if he wanted to change this value or not. Earl asked himself whether the high cost of his excitement was worth it. He weighed the pros and cons of this one value and tried to decide whether to keep it first in his life, to move it down in importance, or to give it up.

values and how they shape your behavior. The best place to look for them is in your past. If the values you say you have seem different from how you live, you are not alone. When sex offenders are asked about their values, they often say they value love, friendship, generosity, and religion—all very positive. Yet their behavior doesn't express these positive values. One man may say he values love, but as soon as things don't go his way he gets angry. Another may say he values friendship, but as soon as his friend doesn't act like he wants he gets rid of him. These men have hidden values, one of which might be "me first." You probably have a case of hidden values when the values you think you hold are not reflected in your actions.

A Changed Man

At some time every sex offender says, "I see the light. I made some bad mistakes, but it will never happen again!" The sex offender often thinks that because he feels this way now, his values have changed and he will act appropriately in the future. While in prison or on probation, many sex offenders think their values have changed and they don't need therapy. This is another thinking defect. No matter how sincere you feel, it's an illusion—your real values haven't changed at all.

Your *behavior* has changed because you are in prison, or you are on probation or parole, and you are forced to live up to the system's values. But when you're out from under the correction department's supervision, back in the old environments and old emotional states, your old habitual values come back, and your old ways of coping with stress return. Your real values have not changed. It takes time and hard work to change values, especially ones that you have built up and reinforced over the last 10 to 40 years.

After a year or so of therapy you may think you understand which values you have held very strongly throughout your life. Later on you will feel that you have changed those old values. You may feel different now, but the values that guided your life when you were acting sexually deviant are still present—they are just hidden. A lifetime of deviant values does not change even after a year of hard work. It takes consistent work for years to change very strongly held values permanently. But in a year or two you can begin to change your values with hard work. The earlier in your life that you start working on yourself, the easier your job will be.

Step by Step

The first step in changing your values is discovering what values you now hold. Your actions over the past few years are the most clear-cut indicators of your current values. If you think you value friendship and are a good friend, see how many friends you have had in recent years. If you value love and think that you are a loving person, consider how much love you have given with little thought of what you want in return. If you value religion, consider how much time you have spent with others of your spiritual belief or how often you have prayed. If you think that you value excitement, notice what you have done to create it in your life. If you value sexuality, consider what you have done to get sex. Look back over all aspects of your life. See what your behavior shows that you value.

In reviewing your behavior it is important not to just look at how you are most of the time, but to look at how you are all of the time. *Three things show how much you value something: how much you would sacrifice for it; how much energy and time you give to it; and how you act when your value is under stress.*

Someone who values friendship helps a friend even when it is inconvenient. You may try to make contact even when he or she appears withdrawn. You might take time away from other important projects to cultivate that friendship. When you have a disagreement you would make efforts to work out your problems with each other. On the other hand, it is easy to value friends when they are generous. It is easy to get along with people when they reach out to you. Saying that you value friendship when your friends are agreeing with you does not tell you how much you value friendship.

The second step in changing values is to realize that you can create new ones. By putting time and energy into a new value, you increase its worth to you. The hard part is how easy it is to forget your new value and fall back into old habits.

It takes determination and commitment over time to create a new value. Consider a car. Just seeing a car on the road doesn't make it valuable to you. If you put money into the car, then it becomes valuable. If you were given a junk car nobody else wanted, it is almost worthless. But when you have cleaned it up and gotten the motor running, it becomes more valuable. You did the work, you made the car valuable by putting time and energy into it. But redoing a car takes a lot of work; it is all too easy to let it sit in the driveway making rust.

Your deviant cycle is made up of steps that you have made valuable by the time and energy you have put into them. Since you have put time and energy into deviant sexuality for years, you have created a strong value. When you put time and energy into getting high, drugs were valuable to you. When you put time and energy into pornography, it became valuable to you.

The good news is that you can establish a healthy value in the same way. When you put time and energy into your spiritual practice, your spirituality becomes valuable. When you put time and energy into staying sober, your sobriety becomes valuable to you. An offender who puts time and energy into becoming mentally healthy and overcoming his deviance makes his recovery valuable.

Chapter 5 Assignments
∽ Do not write in this workbook ∽

16. Take a piece of paper and draw a line down through the center of the page. On one side write "NEGATIVE VALUES," and on the other side write "POSITIVE VALUES." Write out the positive and negative values that you feel you have in your life. Consider especially what you have done in your life, what values you have had about work, relationships, children, money, sex, drugs, cars, travel, excitement, etc. To do this assignment well, you must have at least 30 values on your list.

17. Review your life and make a list of 20 people. For each person consider how the values you listed in Assignment #16 affected your relationship. Were you friendly, generous, forgiving, selfish, blaming, angry, etc. Estimate what you did or did not value by looking at how you behaved in your relationships with those 20 people.

18. What parts of your personality have you valued in the past? Divide another piece of paper. Head one side with the words "GOOD VALUES" and the other side with "BAD VALUES." Using the same format write out what you think you have valued about the positive and negative parts of your own personality.

19. Divide another page down the center. On one side write "VALUES MY PAST SHOWS" and on the other side write "VALUES I WANT IN THE FUTURE." Write out your past and future values for the following words. Rate each value on a 10-point scale. Rate the value a one (1) if it is not very valuable and a ten (10) if it is very valuable. GIVE AN EXAMPLE OF EACH VALUE, one for your past and one for your future:

success	work	sleep	exercise	excitement
sex	fellatio	cunnilingus	children	money
therapy	wife or womanfriend	cars	house	alcohol
gambling	drugs	religion	ministers	friendship
murder	rape	child molesting	love	food
prison	AA	education	driving	lying
TV	government	politicians	women	guards
movies	violence	security	reading	art
music	stability	faithfulness		

Example:

VALUES MY PAST SHOWS

DRUGS, (rate____)
    I have spent all my paycheck on drugs leaving bills unpaid

SEX, (rate ____)
    I have spent many hours cruising for prostitutes

SUCCESS, (rate ____)
    I worked very long hours to make my business succeed

VALUES I WANT IN THE FUTURE

SOBRIETY, (rate ____)
    I want to put time and energy into staying clean and sober.

FAMILY, (rate ____)
    I will make sure that my family's needs come first.

Review these assignments with your therapist and with your group. If you are working on your own, share them with a friend or person you trust.

6.

Links and Chains that Maintain Your Cycle

IN PREVIOUS CHAPTERS YOU LEARNED about the parts of the cycle. In this chapter you will learn how the parts interact as *links* and *chains* to make up the cycle. Remember, the *cycle* is a series of behaviors where the end of the last series is linked to the beginning of the first series, automatically repeating the whole pattern. The cycle is different from a *chain*: a cycle is longer, more complex, and repeats itself automatically; a chain is usually shorter, simpler, and does not repeat itself automatically. Cycles are made up of chains that are linked together. The connections between the chains may be *thoughts*, *feelings*, or *actions*.

Links

Links are the hooks of chains and cycles. They connect one part of a chain with another. They are simple, often appear insignificant, and yet are vital.

There are two types of links: *behavioral links* and *connector links*. A *behavioral link* is a behavior that naturally follows another behavior and leads to the next behavior. For example, chewing naturally follows putting food in your mouth and leads to swallowing. Chewing is the link that connects the act of putting food in your mouth with the act of swallowing.

Connector links are the thoughts and/or feelings that always occur before and after a behavior link. They usually begin and end a chain. The thought, "I'll get some ice cream," is an example of a connector link. It links together "feeling hungry" and "going to the refrigerator." If you felt hungry but did not think of getting something to eat, it is unlikely that you would "go to the refrigerator."

Each individual link is also connected to what you do next. The thinking link, "I'll get some ice cream" is linked to "eating" by the behavior "going to the refrigerator." When you think of your behavior as a series of links you start noticing links everywhere. Sitting down is a natural link between getting a book and reading.

Behaviors are perhaps the strongest links. Small behaviors often begin old patterns of thinking, feeling, and perception. Buying pornography

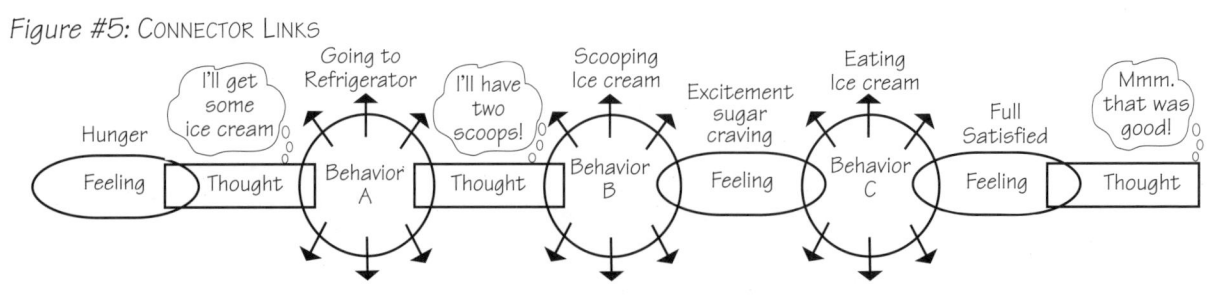

Figure #5: CONNECTOR LINKS

CONNECTOR LINKS ARE THOUGHTS AND FEELINGS THAT ALWAYS OCCUR BEFORE AND AFTER A BEHAVIOR

influences your thoughts, how you feel, and what you see. What you think, feel, and see affects what you do. Behaviors that are links in your cycle can be as obvious as stomping out of the house and slamming the door, or they may be as subtle as *not* talking or *not* telling the truth.

The Stimulus-Response Connection

Each link is composed of a *stimulus* and a *response*. A stimulus is a starting event: a perception (something you see, hear, touch, taste, or smell); a thought (a fantasy, an idea, or a question); a feeling (like anger, sadness, or grief); or a situation (like encountering a woman with a stalled car). Whatever the *stimulus* (or *starting* event) is, some *response* (a *following* event) immediately comes after it. A response might be another thought, another feeling, or some action (see Figure #6). For example, if you have a thought about going out for ice cream (a *starting* event) your response might be to check your pocket to see if you have any money (a *following* event).

Another example of a stimulus would be seeing an ad on TV for a hamburger. Your response might be noticing you are hungry and going to the kitchen to see what there is to eat. Every time there is a stimulus, there is a response. Some responses are regular—you can count on them. For example, you see your favorite hamburger place and (if you're hungry) you think of food. Other responses are not usual, like seeing the moon and singing "God Bless America".

Responses you have only once in a great while are unlikely to become habits. Your regular, predictable responses, those that seem "caused" by an event, are the important ones.

Predictable responses do not just happen. They are created over time. For example, imagine that you are a 12-year-old out for a drive with your parents. You happen to see a girl (a *stimulus*). You think, "She's nice, I'd like to meet her" (a *response*). You have formed a link. For a 12-year-old this is a very weak link; it is not automatic. Now think about yourself as that 12-year-old grown up into an adult. While out driving, you see a woman and you *automatically* size her up, deciding how attractive she is. This link is now very strong because you have reinforced it over many years; it is very predictable.

The more times you create the same link, the stronger that link becomes. You make each link by how you behave. For example, the first time that you look at pornography (a *stimulus*) you might have a brief flash of a sexual thought (a *response*). But after you make this link many times it becomes very strong; just a glance may lead to intense and prolonged sexual thoughts and feelings.

Sometimes the response to an event is predictable and causally related, as when tapping a typewriter key with your finger. You tap the key (the *stimulus*) and the resulting character (the *response*) is clear, predictable, and obviously related to the finger tap. Sometimes the response

Figure #6: STIMULUS-RESPONSE

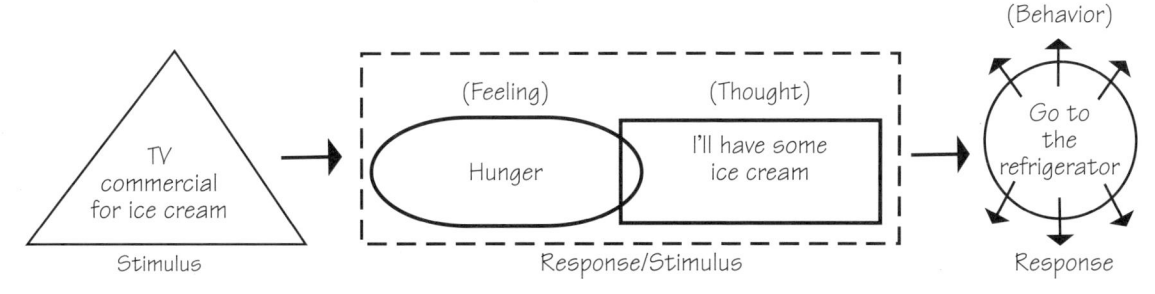

EACH LINK IS COMPOSED OF A "STIMULUS" AND A "RESPONSE"

is unclear. For instance, when you think about leaving work (the *stimulus*), at different times you respond with different thoughts or actions: "It is not time yet," you think; or "They'll dock my pay, I can't afford it"; or you leave. In all three responses the *stimulus* (thought) came before and influenced the behavioral *response* which followed (leaving work or staying at work).

Each link of the chain or cycle is a stimulus that leads to a response. Each response becomes the stimulus for the next link. The links of the cycle might interact like this:

Figure #7: LINKS OF A CYCLE

Stimulus ———> Response/Stimulus ———> Response/Stimulus ———> Response/Stimulus ———> Response/Stimulus ———> Response ———>

In this way the chain of behavior—and the cycle—is built one link at a time. Each link starts some activity (a *stimulus*) and ends with some result (a *response*). That response becomes the new stimulus for the next response.

The exact relationship you form between a stimulus and a response may be unique to you or it may be common to many men. An example of an unusual link is when a man's sexual arousal is linked to women's garments or shoes. Men who have a shoe fetish, where shoes are the *stimulus* for sexual thoughts and feelings, have created it over a period of time by masturbating first to fantasies of women's feet and gradually changing the focus of their fantasy to shoes. Masturbation to fantasy is the usual way men link their sexual arousal to deviant behavior. Rapists form links in their chain of deviant behavior by masturbating to fantasies about violent sex. Pedophiles made links that led to their sexual crimes by masturbating to fantasies about sex with young girls and/or boys.

Another aspect of the stimulus-response relationship is the nature of the stimulus. Some stimuli easily lead to certain responses. Ice cream can be easily linked to a sense of pleasure and anticipation. There is a direct and strong relationship between the ice cream (the stimulus) and pleasure (the response). On the other hand, the stimulus "ice cream" does not easily lead to thoughts of violent sex, since they are not naturally connected. Likewise, because of the differing degree of natural connection between them, fantasies of eating large amounts of vegetables are not easily linked to thoughts of masturbation. But viewing small amounts of pornography easily leads to masturbation, since pornography is about sexual fantasies.

Many offenders' cycles show clear responses to certain stimuli. You can discover relationships between stimuli and your own problem behaviors by observing your behavior and remembering what you did just before it. For example, think about a particular time you looked sexually at a child, and ask yourself, "What did I do just before thinking of sex?" By carefully examining your thoughts and behavior you may discover what triggers your deviant fantasy.

You can also learn about the stimulus-response links in your cycle by looking at your history and listening to others' experiences. Some links form very easily in an offender's cycle: drugs —> violence; wanting to feel powerful —> dominating women; X-rated movies —> prostitutes; loneliness —> prostitutes; anger —> sexual violence, etc.

Discovering Your Cycle's Links

When looking at your cycle it is important to notice even the smallest links. Notice your *consistent* responses. For example, if you frequently get hungry while watching TV and head for the refrigerator, watching TV may be a link in a chain that leads to your overeating. You can tell it is a link by the consistency of the response. Once you discover the link, you can plan how to break it. You might limit your TV watching, or keep junk food out of the house when football season starts.

Another example would be noticing that you get emotionally overwhelmed (one link) and then that you feel tired (a second link). When you are tired, you may find that you want to leave and go to sleep (a third link). Another example of the connection between a stimulus and a response would be noticing that whenever you get criticized (a stimulus), you feel angry (a response). Any time a feeling or behavior happens regularly after a stimulus, it means you have made a strong link in your behavior cycle. As you think about your life, look closely and find the links in your cycle of behavior.

Sometimes men look at their cycles and say they can't find any consistent links. There are three possibilities: they are not paying attention; they haven't completely disclosed their histories; or they have more than one response to a stimulus. If you're denying that you have a problem, or if you're not making an effort, you're not ready to do this work and change your deviant behavior.

You may have several different responses coming from one stimulus. It's like a path that has one starting place then branches two or three times, each branch ending up at a different place. In the same way a certain stimulus may lead to several different branches each ending up in a different place. Boredom often leads to eating, but it may also lead to watching TV or restless, aimless driving. Each outcome is one link in a cycle of behaviors. Each link is connected to several others, with several different paths to the same result (see Figure #8).

When you understand the links in the cycle and how they connect (interlock), the cycle makes sense. Men who come into therapy saying, "I don't know how it happened," often discover that they do know how they took one small step, and how that step led to another small step. When you clearly understand each step you took, you'll know the answer to "Why did I do it again?"

To learn the links in your cycle, start with your typical behaviors, the things you find yourself doing frequently. Once you have identified your behaviors, ask yourself, "What do I generally do just before I do this?" Look at the outcome (the

Figure #8: DEVIANT PATHS

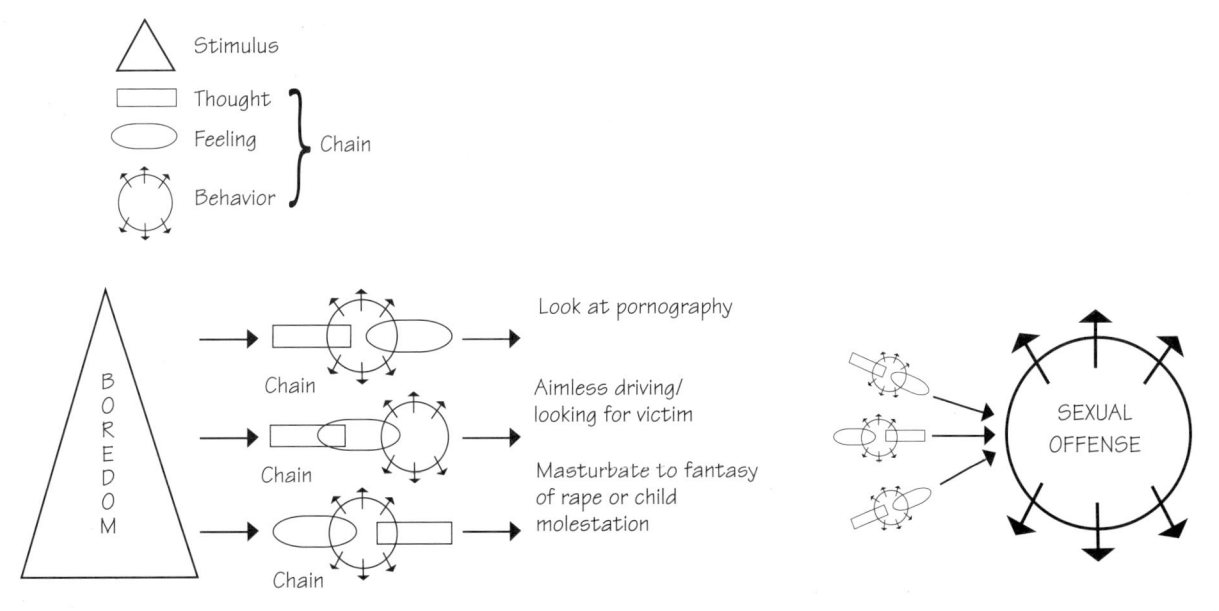

△ Stimulus
▭ Thought
⬭ Feeling   } Chain
⊕ Behavior

Boredom → Chain → [thought/feeling/behavior] → Look at pornography
→ Chain → [thought/feeling/behavior] → Aimless driving/looking for victim
→ Chain → [thought/feeling/behavior] → Masturbate to fantasy of rape or child molestation

→ SEXUAL OFFENSE

EACH LINK IS CONNECTED TO SEVERAL OTHERS; THERE MAY BE SEVERAL DIFFERENT PATHS TO THE SAME RESPONSE

response) and figure out the stimulus that came before it. The behavior chain should begin to make sense to you.

Links Create a Chain

A series of *links* that are repeated become interlocked and form a *chain* of behavior. When a behavior first begins, the response may be unpredictable. For example, the first time you saw pornography you may have felt embarrassed, guilty, or excited. Later, after you'd seen a lot of pornography, your response was more and more predictable, probably masturbation. The more times the series of links are interlocked, the more predictable the response. It's like walking across a field. The first time you walk across it there is no obvious path and you could take any route. When you walk on the same path enough times the grass dies and the path becomes well defined. The path can be compared to the chain. The links are the steps that we take to go from one end of the path to the other. Each step is essential. Initially you don't know where the steps may lead, but later each step leads you down the chain's predictable path.

Thoughts, feelings, perceptions, situations, and behaviors all hook into each other to make up behavior chains that can be long or short. It may take many repetitions before they lead to deviant behavior or it may take only one.

Consider how the links of the chain or steps of the path relate to your deviant sexual cycle. Many sexual offenders created a strong chain in their deviant cycle by masturbating to pornography. The first time you looked at a pornographic magazine it may not have led you to deviant sexual thoughts or behavior. Later, after looking at pornography many times, you may have learned to make a strong link between looking at pornography and having sexually deviant fantasies. Still later you may have learned to link deviant fantasies to deviant behaviors such as rape or molesting a child. Each of these relationships became a link in the cycle that leads to a sexual crime.

Habits: Chains You Don't Think About

Habits are well established chains of behavior that are strongly linked to your daily life. You don't have to pay much attention for them to work because they are automatic and predictable. Eventually, behavior chains that are repeated become a habit, like smoking a cigarette. With habits, you do not have to tell yourself to do all of the separate steps—they automatically happen in sequence.

When you smoke you don't consciously think, "Now I am finding my cigarette pack, I am finding my matches, I am lighting my match," etc. It all happens so automatically that while smoking you can think about work and what you need to get accomplished today. In fact, you must make a deliberate and consistent effort to make a permanent difference in your smoking chain.

In most cases a sex offender's deviant cycle is composed of many strong habitual chains. You automatically go into linked behaviors that result in targeting a victim. This may be so automatic that almost before you realize it, you have found a victim and begun the set-up. By then it is often too difficult for you to stop. You perform these habitual behaviors almost as if you are operating on remote control.

Because habits are automatic they are difficult to break. When you try to break them they often come back as soon as your attention shifts away. Breaking a habitual chain requires constant attention and effort because it is linked together so tightly. You don't overcome the habits of smoking, drinking, or sexual deviancy easily. You have to work long and hard on breaking individual links to begin breaking habit chains.

Behavior Chains Link Into a Cycle

A *chain* is a series of behaviors that follow one after another. A *cycle* consists of a pattern of behavior where the end hooks into the beginning and the whole pattern repeats itself automatically. It is easy to add a chain on to a pre-existing cycle. Your body automatically needs to eat and sleep in a cycle. Many chains of behavior are added on to your basic biological cycles of eating and sleeping.

An example of a cycle with a chain of behavior added on is the daily pattern you go through when you smoke a cigarette. For most smokers, cigarette smoking is an addiction that has a variety of chains linked together within the daily cycle: the *smoking chain*.

> The smoker decides to have a cigarette. He checks his pockets, finds the package and pulls it out. He opens it, pulls out a cigarette, and taps it on the pack. He reaches for his matches or finds a lighter. He puts the cigarette in his mouth and lights it. He puts the pack of cigarettes and matches back in his pocket.

The smoker practices this chain of behaviors over and over. It becomes automatic: after he decides to have a cigarette, all the other behaviors happen without any thought.

The *hunger cycle* might look like this on any given day:

> feel hungry —> eat —> feel full —> digest —> wait —> feel hungry —> eat —> feel full —> digest —> wait —> feel hungry —> etc.

Often the *smoking chain* is linked into the *hunger cycle*. When the smoker finishes eating, he feels relaxed and thinks a cigarette would be nice. When the *smoking chain* and the *hunger cycle* are put together they look like this:

> Feel hungry —> eat breakfast —> feel full —> smoke chain —> digest —> wait —> feel hungry —> eat lunch —> feel full —> smoke chain —> digest —> wait —> feel hungry —> eat dinner —> feel full —> smoke chain —> etc.

Now you can see how smoking becomes part of a cycle. Every time the smoker eats he starts his smoking chain. The cycle gets more complicated when a *tension trigger* also starts the smoking chain:

> The smoker is talking with a friend and they begin discussing some problems. He begins to get anxious and irritable and more tense as they talk (*the tension trigger*).
>
> He remembers that he feels relaxed when he smokes a cigarette. He enters into the smoke chain.

When this element is added to the smoker's day it might look something like this:

> Wakes up —> hunger cycle —> smoke chain —> goes to work —> every time he talks to boss, customers, or co-workers —> tension trigger —> smoke chain —> hunger cycle —> smoke chain —> every time he talks to boss, customers, or co-workers —> tension trigger —> smoke chain —> goes home —> talks to wife —> tension trigger —> smoke chain —> etc.

The smoker may add a fourth element to this cycle, the *coffee chain*.

> During the day the smoker's mouth gets dry. When he notices it he thinks, "How about a cup of coffee?" He goes to the coffee pot, picks up his cup, pours coffee, sets his cup down, adds cream and sugar, stirs and sips to taste. He drinks his cup of coffee while talking. He also drinks coffee during meals.

When this chain is added together with the feeling trigger (tension) and the smoke chain, you start to have a cycle that is composed of a series of chains.

> Wakes up —> hunger cycle (breakfast) —> coffee chain —> smoke chain —> goes to work —> coffee chain —> talks —> tension —> smoke chain —> hunger cycle (lunch) —> smoke chain —> coffee chain —> talks —> tension —> smoke chain —> coffee chain —> goes home —> talks to wife —> tension —> smoke chain —> hunger cycle (dinner) —> coffee chain —> smoke chain —> etc.

As you can see from these examples, chains of behavior can follow one another and become linked together. When they are linked together and repeat themselves they become a cycle (see Figure #9).

Some Basic Cycles

Typical activities that demonstrate a simple cycle might include: work, depression, anger, and masturbation. If you are a workaholic, you might have the following cycle with work:

1. You feel *almost normal*. You have a low level of frustration or boredom, which leads to ...
2. *Anxiety* about money or success. Your responsibilities start to weigh on you. The cycle starts to build up and may continue to build over the next days or weeks. During this time you find yourself beginning to work faster, longer, and harder. You may take on an extra job or start working more overtime without giving yourself time to recover, which leads to ...
3. The *Acting-out* phase. During this stage, a workaholic starts getting angry at co-workers.

Figure #9: CHAINS BECOME A CYCLE

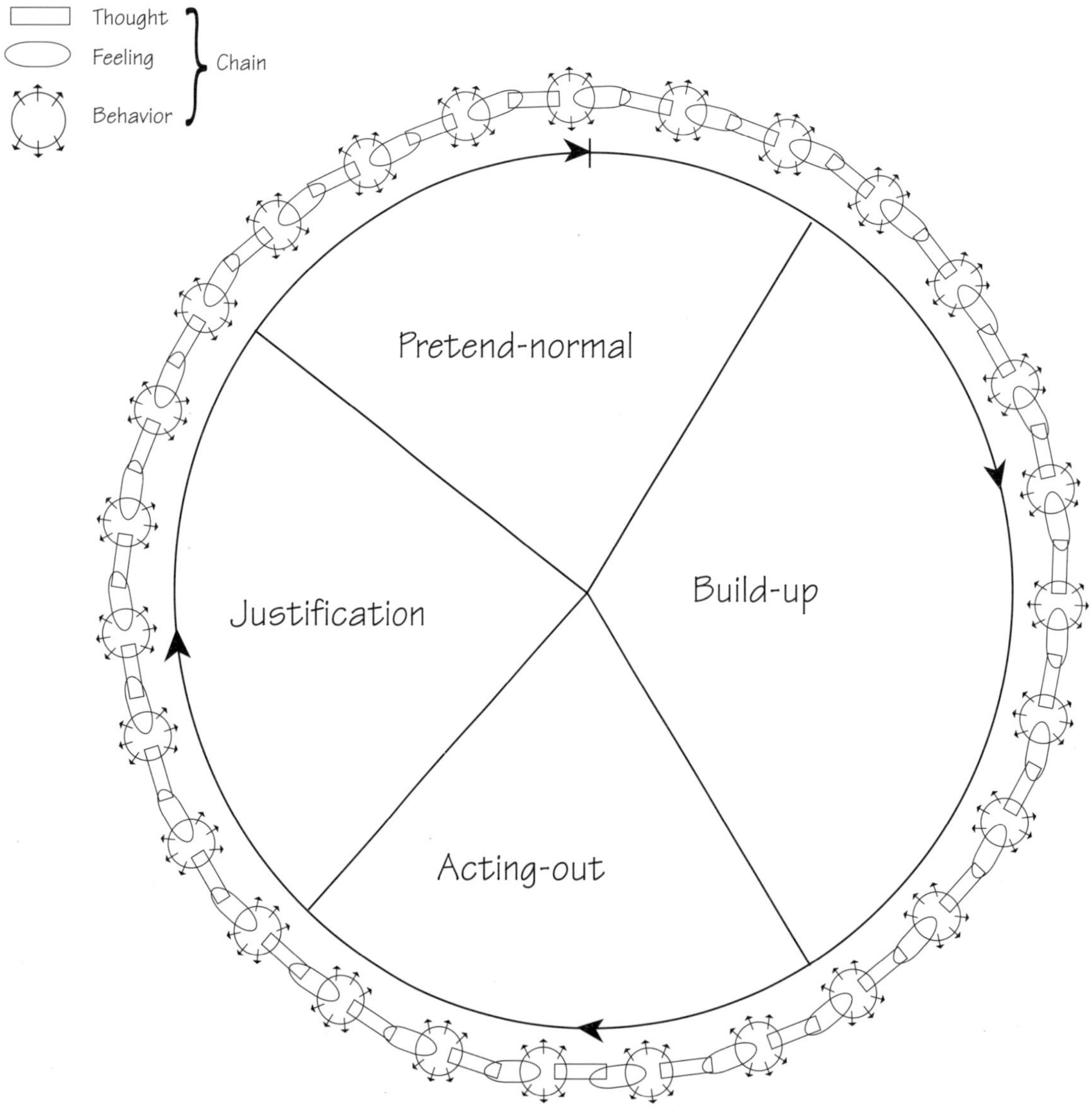

□ Thought
○ Feeling   } Chain
⊛ Behavior

Pretend-normal

Build-up

Acting-out

Justification

You become very demanding while blaming others. You start drinking as an escape from the pressure. By now you are working at an incredible pace, over-committed and failing to complete all of the tasks that you have set yourself up for, which leads to ...

4. <u>Burn-out</u> (the same as the Justification phase in the deviant cycle). You are totally exhausted and feel like a failure. Often you are very depressed and don't feel like you can do anything. Everything stops: you look at your life and wonder what went wrong, despite all your hard work. You vow to do better next time (meaning that you will try to work even harder), which leads to ...

5. The <u>Pretend-normal</u> phase. When you finally have recovered enough physically and psychologically to be able to work, you feel almost normal and start the cycle all over again.

The pattern of this cycle is:

Feeling inadequate —> overworking —> frustration —> exhaustion —> Feeling inadequate —> overworking —> frustration —> exhaustion —> Feeling inadequate —> overworking —> frustration —> etc.

If you have a cycle of masturbation, it might follow a pattern like this:

1. You feel a <u>lack</u>—some sort of boredom, frustration, or restlessness. You begin to <u>fantasize</u> about doing something that feels good.
2. You pick up some <u>pornography</u>, look at it and imagine having sex. If a sexual partner is unavailable, you may decide to <u>masturbate</u> instead. If masturbating feels good, you start to look for <u>more pornography</u> to masturbate with whenever you feel uncomfortable.
3. While <u>masturbating</u> the uncomfortable feelings disappear, but after you finish, you start <u>feeling low</u> again and the uncomfortable feelings return. When you feel <u>guilty</u> about masturbating, you may feel worse than when you started.
4. You know that if you <u>masturbate</u> again the guilty feelings go away for a while. Once again you start looking for <u>pornography</u> ...

The pattern of this cycle is:

feeling uptight —> pornography —> masturbation —> guilt —> feeling uptight —> pornography —> masturbation —> guilt —> feeling uptight —> pornography —> masturbation —> etc.

These examples show two very simple cycles. Each of us has many different cycles in our lives, some much longer and more complex than these. Some are very strong and some are weak. If a cycle is very strong, like a habit, then it continues until it wears itself out, is stopped by an external force, or you intervene and stop it.

Breaking a Cycle

You can interrupt negative cycles of behavior. You stop a cycle by breaking its links. What you consciously use to break a negative cycle is called an "intervention." You can intervene in the pornography/masturbation cycle in many ways: by learning relaxation techniques or how to meditate when you get uptight; by getting rid of all pornography in your environment; by calling up a friend and telling him or her that you need to talk. Any of these actions would break the cycle and stop the behavior. Stopping a behavior so it never returns means intervening many, many times.

Interventions in a cycle can be positive and productive. Calling up a friend is a positive way to intervene in the pornography/masturbation cycle because it helps reduce the stress and leaves you feeling better.

To break a deviant cycle, you have to attack the individual chains of behavior. In order to break a chain you have to work on undoing the links. There is an old saying, "A chain is only as strong as its weakest link." But for addictions and habits it works just the opposite: the habit chain is as strong as the strongest link. Each link of the chain must be looked at and broken to break a habitual chain. Breaking just one link is not enough. Consider Rick who has anger problems:

Raging Rick

Rick gets so angry that he hits his wife and children. In talking with his therapist he has become aware of a pattern.

First, at work he thinks that jobs must be done exactly as he says. When he sees them done differently he gets frustrated and angry. Second, after work he is tense from all his frustration and thinks a few beers will relax him. In the bar he gets into several arguments. He leaves still frustrated. Third, he goes home and notices a number of little things that he thinks his wife or children have done wrong. He feels irritated and demands they do things the way he wants them done. Fourth, when his family resists, he insists on showing them who is the boss. Fifth, he gets into a heated argument and hits them.

Rick obviously has a problem with his anger. There are a number of links in his chain of behaviors. If Rick broke one of the links it would help, but breaking one link would probably not be enough to break his anger/violence chain. Rick could break the "going into the bar and drinking" link; stopping his drinking might help him not get so violently angry. He'd be sober, but he would still feel frustrated and angry; he would still be demanding and looking for a fight.

He will have to break several links to break the chain of behaviors that led up to hitting his wife and children. In addition to breaking the bar/drinking link, he'll have to break the thought links ("my way is the only way") that led to his frustration, or the feeling links ("I'm afraid no one respects me; I'm angry they think I'm stupid") that feed his need to have it out with his family, to be the boss all the time.

For a strong behavior chain you must break links of many different types, including thoughts, feelings, behaviors, and situations. Situations and environments affect how we think, feel, and act. Going to a bar or stopping by a liquor store are two possible links between the thought "I'll have a drink" and the behavior of "drinking." Break the environmental link by not going into the store or the bar, and you break the chain.

How you live, whom you associate with, and what kind of work you do affect your cycle. If you are a spiritual man with good moral values and you spend time with like-minded people, you make healthy links that help you to think and act more like them. If you are a drug addict and you spend time with other drug addicts you act more like them. Whom you choose to be with, where you choose to be with them, and what usually happens in that environment are some of the factors that link thoughts, feelings, and perceptions.

Chapter 6 Assignments

◈ Do not write in this workbook ◈

20. Explain how environment effects your cycles. Why is the environment where you choose to live, work, and socialize so important in helping you not reoffend?

21. List all the habits that you have. Include habits of behavior, habits of thought, and habits of feeling. You should identify at least 10 to 20 habits.

22. Write down and describe a cycle (other than your deviant sexual cycle) that uses a habit. The habit that you use may be either a good one or a bad one. Write down the cycle of this habit. Using the cycle theory that you have learned, describe how you would begin to break the habit.

23. What is meant by stimulus and response? Give ten (10) examples out of your life that show a stimulus-response connection.

24. Explain why you can do one behavior one time and it will end in one result and then the next time you do it, it may end in a different result.

25. Therapists who work with sex offenders usually give you several instructions about what to do or not do. Some of these instructions might be:
    For Rapists:
    1. Do not take your car out for aimless drives.
    2. Do not drive where there are prostitutes.
    3. Do not walk alone late at night.
    4. Do not take a job that requires door-to-door sales.
    For Child Molesters:
    1. Do not ever be alone with any child.
    2. Do not walk through video arcades or parks.
    3. Do not date women who have young children.
    4. Do not work at a job or engage in activities which will bring you into contact with lots of children such as teaching school or Sunday school classes, Boy Scouts, driving a school bus, etc.

    Pick one set of these instructions. Use what you know about cycles, chains, and links to explain why these instructions are given.

26. Now that you understand much more about how the cycle works, look at your big diagram of your deviant cycle. Add more detail to it. When you complete this you will have several steps of the cycle, some chains in the cycle, and some links. Be sure to include environments, feelings, thoughts, behaviors, and triggers.

Review these assignments with your therapist and with your group. If you are working on your own, share the assignments with a friend or person you trust.

PART II THE CYCLE

7.
Your Deviant Cycle: Putting It All Together

ONCE YOU HAVE FULLY DISCLOSED all the details of your crime, understanding your deviant cycle is the next most important part of treatment. Deviant behaviors like molesting children or raping people do not just spontaneously happen without other behaviors leading up to them. In order to learn how to intervene effectively and stop these behaviors from occurring, you must understand the details of every part of your deviant cycle. When you understand the steps you took, you can effectively intervene and stop the cycle.

Phases of the Cycle

A typical deviant sexual cycle for an offender might look like this:

> Boredom —> Fantasy about pleasure/excitement —> Building sexual interest (often with pornography) —> Planning the sexual assault —> Commitment to do the assault —> The sexual assault —> Fear and guilt —> Rationalization (or other defense mechanisms) —> Vowing never to do it again —> Working hard to make up for the deviant behavior —> Return to daily routine —> Boredom —> etc.

Notice that this cycle has several parts:

1. It has a period of *Build-up*, including:

> Fantasy about pleasure/excitement —> Building sexual interest (often with pornography) —> Planning the sexual assault —> Commitment to do the assault.

2. Next, it has a long or short period of *Acting-out*. Here is where the worst part of your deviant sexual cycle happens:

> The sexual assault. (In this phase some sexual offenders act out many deviant behaviors over a short time. For example, a peeping Tom may act out only a few times a year, but when he does, he peeps many times a week.)

3. Next, the cycle has a *Justification* phase, including:

> Fear and guilt —> Rationalization (or other defense mechanisms that are used to deny the problem) —> Vowing never to do it again.

4. Then, it has a *Pretend-normal* phase, including:

> Working hard to make up for the deviant behavior —> Return to daily routine —> Boredom —> etc.

In some cases the four phases of the cycle occur repeatedly and quickly, maybe even in a single day. The example above is a streamlined and shortened version of the whole cycle. But in real life the cycle may take weeks or even months to build to a sexual assault. Consider Hank, a guy whose cycle is sexually deviant. Hidden in his story are the cycles, chains, and links that make up his deviant sexual cycle. See if you can identify the parts of the cycle and understand how each step of the cycle follows the preceding one:

Horny Hank

Hank is a successful 42-year-old businessman who loves his wife, has an interesting job, and has three children. Hank's job requires that he travel in and out of state at least twice a month. He has an expense account for food, lodging, and travel. Additionally, Hank earns a commission every time he makes a sale while on the road.

At home Hank spends a lot of money on pornography. He buys it secretly and hides the expense from his wife. Each day he spends time looking at his collection, and every week he buys more magazines or X-rated movies. He keeps pornography in his car and at the office, and he masturbates once or twice a day after looking at it. He keeps his behavior very secretive and discreet. Hank has sex with his wife three-to-four times a week, but he feels it is not enough. He says this is one of the reasons he uses pornography.

While on the road, Hank works hard and puts in extra hours to make a sale. He considers the extra sales commission his "sex money." When away from home Hank buys more pornography, watches pornographic movies, and hires prostitutes for sex.

From the time he wakes up in the morning until he falls asleep at night, Hank routinely thinks about making more money so he can have more sex. He imagines how exciting it will be to get some new, more thrilling pornography. On his way to work he drives by adult book stores, thinking and fantasizing about what they have that may be newer and better than what he has. When he goes home from work Hank stops at a topless bar for a drink, looks at the dancers, and fantasizes about having sex with them. When a business trip comes up, Hank begins to plan for having sex with a prostitute.

On one business trip Hank hits the hotel, goes straight for the phone book, looks up escort services, calls a service, and asks them to send a woman over later. When his work day is done, Hank skips dinner and goes back to his room to get ready for his "date." When she arrives Hank tells her he would like to have sex with her and they agree on the price. The woman turns out to be a police officer and arrests him. He is horrified, terrified that his wife or boss might find out. Hank is kept overnight at the police station; in the morning he is cited and fined.

After he returns from the trip Hank is depressed. He feels guilty about being unfaithful to his wife, spending the family's money and wasting time that could be spent with his family. Hank thinks about what he has done. He vows to overcome his addiction to sex. Hank is depressed about his problem and feels confused and hopeless about his situation. He is also horrified at how much he has done over the years to support his addiction.

But when Hank gets home he lies to his wife about his trip, covers up the lost money, and pretends that nothing has happened. Hank vows again that he will take care of the problem. He gives up pornography and throws his expensive collection away. Hank promises himself that he will not have sex with anyone but his wife and that he will work hard to remake the money that he has wasted.

After a few months without pornography or prostitutes, he thinks, "I'm doing pretty well now. I don't have to be so careful. He starts thinking about pornography and says, "Well, just this once." Hank tells himself, "I can do this if I do it in moderation. Other men do this, so why can't I?" Soon he is deep in his cycle again. His addiction to sex is so strong that it governs his behavior both at home and on the road. After years of this, Hank knows that "willpower" alone is not enough. But he has been afraid to get into treatment because someone else will find out about his problem, and Hank is afraid of feeling humiliated. Hank's sexual addiction costs him a minimum of $400 per month, plus the costs for his criminal charges.

This example is complex, containing several cycles, some chains, and many links. Let's dissect and expand this example in order to take a closer look at what Hank is doing. There are a great many links in this example, but we point out only a few.

The *Build-up* phase of a small cycle:

Hank wakes up every day, notices how his penis feels (a stimulus) and starts thinking about sex (a response). As he thinks about sex he starts to feel aroused (another stimulus and response). By the time Hank leaves for work he has decided to drive by an adult book store (a thinking link between leaving home and driving to the pornography shop).

While driving, Hank reaches under his seat and pulls out the pornography that he keeps in his car (another link, i.e., having pornography in his car makes it easier for Hank to stay aroused, and helps him justify buying more). He tells himself, "This magazine is boring, it's been in the car too long," and gives himself permission to buy more pornography.

Hank not only feels aroused but thinks to himself, "Maybe I'll buy that expensive French pornography today." Once he has decided to buy the pornography he justifies his purchase by thinking, "I've been working so hard, I deserve some pleasure."

At this point Hank enters a short *Acting-out* phase.

He stops off and spends $35 on what he thinks will be a very classy new magazine. He sits in his car in the parking lot, looking at the magazine and masturbating (buying the pornography is a link between driving to work and arriving at work distracted and inattentive).

Now Hank enters the *Justification* phase.

By the time Hank reaches work he is late and feels guilty for wasting his time and money. Hank lies to his boss about why he is late and then works in a frenzy to try to catch up. Sexually excited and distracted by thoughts of pornography, he takes much longer than usual to get organized and does not do a good job. He tells himself that he will never let sex interfere with work again.

Next Hank enters the *Pretend-normal* phase.

By lunch time Hank has calmed down, gotten his mind on his work and has worked productively for a couple of hours. He thinks that he is back to normal. He has forgotten his guilt and his promises.

Hank now starts a new mini-cycle with a new *Build-up* phase.

During his lunch break, Hank remembers the pornography in his desk. He says to himself that a quick look won't hurt anything (starting the cycle over again). He takes the pornography out of his desk drawer and looks at it. He starts to feel aroused (a link between looking at pornography and the next thoughts). He thinks, "Soon I will be going on a trip and maybe I will find a woman who looks as good as the ones in the magazine," heightening his arousal.

Hank now enters the second *Acting-out* phase.

His sexual feelings are now intense. Hank decides that he can't stand it and goes into the bathroom to masturbate (acting out).

Once more Hank starts the *Justification* phase of the cycle.

After his orgasm, someone knocks on the bathroom door. Realizing it would look bad if someone found him, Hank gets scared and feels out of control. Just this morning he promised himself he wouldn't let sex interfere with work again. He leaves, feels guilty, and spends half the afternoon worrying about his problem. Gradually he makes himself feel okay. He swears again that he will handle it this time.

Hank enters the *Pretend-normal* phase.

Gradually he relaxes and once again gets to work. He tries to work hard to make up for his previous poor performance. His cycle continues on and on and on ...

Hank builds up his deviant cycle by using a number of thoughts, feelings, perceptions, and behaviors to form the links that make him feel more sexually aroused and lead to deviant behavior: Hank wakes and lets his mind dwell on sex; he leaves the house knowing he is going to drive by the adult book stores; he has been thinking about sex from the time he woke up; he looks at the magazine in his car and thinks about buying another; he looks at the pornography, masturbates, then goes out and buys more pornography.

There are thinking links in the chain of Hank's behaviors. He begins his day by thinking about pornography and buying more. He thinks about masturbating to it, does so, thinks about buying more, and makes a commitment to do so.

Feeling links centered around Hank's sexual arousal are connected to his thinking. Hank begins feeling sexually aroused, becomes excited, and then feels physical and mental urges to masturbate and maintain his sexual excitement. Hank's thoughts and feelings are links in his chain of behaviors that result in a cycle of addictive sexual excitement and ritual behavior.

Behaviors fill in the gaps in the cycle. Driving by the adult book stores, going in, looking at magazines, having pornography in his car, driving by the porno shops, taking his new purchase into his office, and hiding in the bathroom to masturbate are all behaviors Hank uses to keep his deviant cycle going.

Every time Hank goes through his cycle it becomes a bit harder to stop. Each time, the cycle goes a bit faster and gets more intense.

The Intensifying Cycle

The pattern that was just discussed is Hank's typical cycle. Some days, though, Hank goes more deeply into his deviant cycle. Instead of the cycle peaking after he masturbates, the *Build-up* phase continues.

> After masturbating at work Hank is satisfied for a while. Later that day Hank has a few idle minutes and he starts thinking about what he has seen in the magazine. He gets turned on and thinks, "Maybe there will be a new topless dancer that looks like that woman in the magazine. I'll check out the bar after work." After work Hank stops by the topless bar, has a drink, and fantasizes that the prostitute he will hire next week will look like the girl dancing on the stage. Hank puts dollar bills in her g-string as she dances in front of him and his sexual arousal intensifies.

Hank is now even more wound up and turned on. He is ready to enter the *Acting-out* phase again.

> When she is done dancing Hank sneaks outside and looks for the dancers' entrance. He starts thinking that he may be able to meet her in private. He sneaks in the door and starts checking out the dressing rooms. But as soon as he is inside he is seen by a woman who angrily starts to come towards him. He runs and gets away. Now he is excited with feelings of both fear and sex. He goes to the men's room to masturbate.

Next is the *Justification* phase of the cycle.

> Hank goes back into the bar, his mind a swirl of confused thoughts. He thinks about how late it is and that he needs to go home. Hank feels afraid and stupid about what he just tried to pull. What if the woman had screamed? He also starts worrying about depriving his family of time with him and the money he spends on his sexual addiction. He rationalizes his behavior by thinking, "My wife is probably cooking dinner, and the kids are doing their homework so they won't miss me anyway." Hank tells himself that his wife and kids have everything they need so a few dollars spent on relaxation will not deprive his family.
>
> He then begins to wonder what will happen if someone he knows walks in. What if someone sees him and tells his wife? He moves to a dark corner so he can see who is walking into the bar, but no one can see him. He fears the consequences of his behavior. Hank is late getting home. He has missed dinner with his family because of his drinking and his sexual acting out. He beats himself up mentally for being a horrible father and husband. But then Hank lies and tells his wife and children that he was at a business meeting called at the last minute.

Later Hank talks to himself and convinces himself that everything is all right. He has again entered the *Pretend-normal* phase.

> After lying to his family Hank eats dinner, watches TV, talks with his wife, and puts the kids to bed. He relaxes and begins to forget what happened.

Later that night in bed the *Build-up* phase of the cycle starts again.

> As Hank rests in bed that night, his mind starts racing with thoughts about the pornography he has looked at and purchased today. He thinks about the dancer he has just seen and imagines a woman just like her lying in bed with him. He imagines the prostitute he will hire next week. He wants someone to have sex with right now, but his wife has long since gone to sleep. Discouraged, his thoughts shift back to the dancer as he falls asleep. In the morning he wakes up, becomes aware of his penis, and starts thinking about sex.

Hank's intensifying cycle consists of a chain of behaviors linked by thoughts, feelings, and perceptions. The chain of behaviors is occurring quickly and becoming more intense. Hank ends up feeling frustrated, depressed, and angry with himself for what he has just done. These negative feelings are typical of Hank's cycle and of other cycles like it.

Cycling into Jail

Now Hank's cycle continues to build to greater intensity. He is not just looking at pornography, going to topless shows, and masturbating (things which are not illegal) but he is involving another person in his deviancy. By using a prostitute, Hank is committing an act for which he could be arrested.

> The next week Hank goes on an overnight business trip to a neighboring state. While packing for his trip he makes sure that he has enough cash on hand to pay for the prostitute. When he arrives, he checks into his hotel and calls an escort service asking for a woman to meet him later. Thinking about the dancer he had seen at the bar last week, Hank requests a woman with long dark hair who is very petite with a cute figure. As he talks with the woman he begins to get suspicious, wondering if this is an undercover vice operation which could result in his being arrested. He has a moment of fear but he is so deep in his deviant cycle that he is not thinking clearly enough to pay attention to it. He convinces himself that everything will work out fine; after all, he has done this before and has never been busted. Hank goes to his meeting and works hard at making the sale. As the sale closes, Hank is smiling about having just made the money he needs to make up for what he will spend on the prostitute.
>
> Hank starts to feel sexually excited as he anticipates the evening ahead. While waiting for the prostitute to arrive, he feels guilty about cheating on his wife and gets depressed. He decides to have a drink, and makes himself feel better by telling himself that using a prostitute is helping him keep his marriage together: when he is with a prostitute he is not pressuring his wife for sex all the time. He thinks, "No one is being hurt if she doesn't find out. I will keep my behavior a secret."
>
> There is a knock on the door; it's the prostitute. Hank's heart races and he becomes excited and aroused immediately. When Hank opens the door, he feels disappointed because the woman standing there doesn't look like the woman at the topless bar last week. Despite his disappointment, Hank invites her into his room, thinking to himself, "The next time I hire a prostitute, she will be just like the woman in my fantasy." After they agree on a price for sex, the prostitute turns out to be a police officer. Hank is arrested and cited.

Here you have a larger view of how a deviant cycle works. In Hank's deviant cycle there are also several chains and links which keep his deviant cycle going. Can you identify them? Can you see how they are so woven into Hank's life that they occur day in and day out with everything else he does? Each of these chains is complex, intertwined with other chains, and connected by links.

From Hank's story you can see how intricate just one cycle of behavior can be. It can be so complex that it continues without your awareness of it. Because of its hidden nature, the deviant cycle repeats itself over and over unless you intervene. The more the cycle is repeated, the stronger it becomes. It is important to understand that a very old and strong cycle will not stop by itself. Consider Alan's case.

Angry Alan

Alan is 29 years old. He was in prison once before, doing over six years on a rape charge. While in prison Alan told himself that he would never rape again. He told himself that it was alcohol and drugs that made him act like that. After his release from prison Alan got into a relationship with a woman named Sally and married her. A few months after their marriage, Alan and Sally started having problems. "She doesn't understand all the pressure I'm under," he thought angrily. His anger got in the way of talking with Sally and began affecting his performance at work so much that Alan got fired, putting more financial pressure on their marriage.

Alan and Sally fought over money and his inability to keep a job. To deal with the stress in his life, Alan bought drugs and alcohol with the little money they had. Sally was hurt by seeing their marriage falling apart and Alan on drugs all the time. When Alan was high, he was verbally and physically abusive. Sometimes they physically fought. Several times during these fights, Alan overpowered Sally and forced her to have sex with him (raped her). "She's my wife," he thought, "I've got a right to have sex with her. She owes me my marital rights." Afterward, Sally left and went to her woman friend's house where she felt safe and secure. Alan began to think that she was having an affair with another man over at the woman friend's house, a thought that enraged him even more.

One night while she was gone, Alan committed another rape in a fit of anger. He was caught and sentenced to prison. Sally (who was not having an affair) was shocked to learn her husband was a rapist and divorced Alan immediately.

Again, while in prison, Alan vowed not to rape any more. He hated himself, was depressed, and felt guilty. He kept to himself and played the rape scene over in his mind, trying to understand what had happened. He didn't see himself as a rapist; it was his victims' fault for being alone in their homes with the doors unlocked. In Alan's thinking, they were inviting a man to come in and have sex with them. He told himself that women who don't want sex don't walk around with their doors and windows open.

Alan's thinking while in prison and outside shows several defects here (go back to Chapter Three and use the list of thinking defects to find which ones Alan was using to make himself feel better about what he did). Because of this distorted thinking and the fact that in prison he had no obvious problems, Alan figured that he had changed and was no longer a danger to anyone. He relaxed about his sexual anger problems and got on with his life in prison.

Six months after he was out on parole, Alan was already peeping in windows and targeting victims. He wasn't doing well on his job, he was in debt and stressed out, and he was having problems with his new womanfriend, Carol. Alan began having fantasies of getting her to submit to him. As his fantasies became more violent, so did his fights at home. Alan's fantasies increased until every day was full of rape fantasies. Each time he had a fight with Carol, Alan stomped out of the house and drove aimlessly.

Later Alan started driving around neighborhoods looking for the right house to peep into. One night Alan spotted a woman alone at home who reminded him of Carol. Alan was constantly angry at Carol, thinking she was rejecting him just as Sally had. With his mind full of rape fantasies, he parked his car up the street and crept into the back yard of the woman he had spotted.

Alan watched the woman through a window. As she moved around the house he could feel himself getting sexually aroused. He started thinking about rape. He checked the back door—unlocked. Alan walked in, and, grabbing a pair of scissors off the table, went into the living room and threatened the woman. Alan was raging, determined to make her submit totally to him. He told the woman to shut up and do exactly what he said or he would hurt her.

Once she had shown she would yield, Alan felt anxious and afraid, but told himself that he couldn't back out now. He couldn't get an erection. He was about to force the woman to perform fellatio on him when Alan saw a flash of himself in prison saying he would never do this again. He stopped, told the victim to get dressed, said he was sorry, and ran out of the house.

That evening the police arrested and questioned him. He was sent back to prison. When asked what had happened to all his good intentions, Alan said that he didn't know. He only knew that something had come over him that he just couldn't control.

A Cycle Goes Around

Though Alan's behaviors are different from Hank's, the cycle, chains, and links follow a similar pattern. Hank's cycle has the four typical phases: *Build-up*, *Acting-out*, *Justification*, and *Pretend-normal*. Each of these phases has links and chains. Look over Alan's cycle and try to understand what the parts are and how they fit together.

So far you have learned how cycles work, what they are made of, and the phases they fall into. The next chapter will teach you more about the *Justification* phase.

Chapter 7 Assignments

∞ Do not write in this workbook ∞

27. Write out a deviant cycle that shows how you got into the mind-state of committing your crime using ONLY *events* you experienced and your *reactions* to them. It should look something like this:

    Example:
    1. BUILD-UP PHASE Perception —> Reaction —> Behavior
       climaxing in the ...
    2. ACTING-OUT PHASE Perception —> Reaction —> Behavior
       leading to the ...
    3. JUSTIFICATION PHASE Perception —> Reaction —> Behavior
       and followed again by the ...
    4. PRETEND-NORMAL PHASE Perception —> Reaction —> Behavior

28. Now break your cycle into the four (4) phases and the following steps:

    PHASE 1: PRETEND-NORMAL
    　　A. Part of your normal routine
    　　B. Feelings, thoughts, and behaviors that happen here (i.e., boredom)
    PHASE 2: BUILD-UP
    　　C. Fantasy
    　　D. Sexual urges
    　　E. Planning
    PHASE 3: ACTING-OUT
    　　F. Commitment
    　　G. Assault
    　　H. Other
    PHASE 4: JUSTIFICATION
    　　I. Rationalization
    　　J. Minimization and/or denial
    　　K. Vowing never to do it again
    　　L. Hiding
    　　M. Anger
    　　N. Other
    PHASE 1: PRETEND-NORMAL
    　　A. Part of your normal routine
    　　B. Etc.
    Fill in the cycle with all of the links that you have identified.

Review these assignments with your therapist and with your group. If you are working on your own, share the assignments with a friend or person you trust.

8.
Setting Yourself Up: The Justification Phase

THE FIRST GOAL OF THERAPY is to help you not hurt any more victims. The way that you can do this is to understand how you got yourself into a state of mind to commit a crime. When you really understand this and are motivated to change, you can keep yourself from committing another crime and assaulting more victims.

The work you've done in previous chapters concentrated on the *Build-up* and *Acting-out* phases of your cycle. As you've now learned, the *Build-up* phase includes the emotions, thoughts, environments, and habits that led up to your deviant behavior. The *Acting-out* phase is your sexual assault. In order to stop your cycle of deviance you must now learn about the *Justification* phase, the part of your cycle where you set yourself up to start the cycle over again.

The *Justification* phase includes what happens after you have committed a crime: all the thinking and behaviors you use to try to feel normal, everything you do to lose your awareness of your crime and its impact. Unless you are a sadist, you learned to avoid the awareness of the tremendous pain and confusion you caused, or you wouldn't have acted-out against a second victim. Losing or avoiding this awareness in the *Justification* phase sets the stage for the *Build-up* phase of your next deviant cycle.

Cycles repeat; how they repeat is what the *Justification* phase is all about. This phase of the cycle has many steps, not necessarily in the order that they are listed below. This chapter outlines the common patterns for many sex offenders.

Most sex offenders feel some guilt or shame about their sexually deviant acts, some men more than others. But if your greatest regret is that you got caught; if years of violence have made you unable to feel much of anything; or if you felt elation at how smart you are to have pulled off your previous crimes, some of the steps in the *Justification* phase may not apply to you.

If you are distressed that you have wasted your life by being in prison; if you have ruined a career and wrecked your family; or if you really saw how your actions destroyed your victim's sense of self-esteem and safety; then you probably have felt remorse. If you feel remorse, shame, or sorrow about what your deviance has done to your life and the lives of those around you, this chapter will be meaningful for you. As you read about these steps, think of your own cycle and see what applies to you.

Waking Up

Waking up is what happened immediately after you committed a sexual crime. In order to perform deviant sexual behavior, you probably had to get into some sort of altered state of consciousness. You had to became numb to your feelings and less aware of reality during the *Build-up* phase of the cycle. But after ejaculating or completing a sexual act, you probably felt as though your mind suddenly cleared and you "woke up" to "discover" what you were doing. Some men describe suddenly becoming aware of *how* deviant their behavior is. The *waking-up* stage of *Justifi-*

cation was a short one. It very quickly passed on to the next stage.

Fear

Fear is the emotion most offenders feel after committing a sexual crime. Adrenalin rushed through your body, preparing you to fight or run. "Oh my God! What have I done," you thought, not out of compassion or concern for the victim, but from fear of being caught. Thoughts raced through your mind: "Will they talk, will they turn me in, will they report the crime, did they see me, did I leave any identification, am I carrying anything that could connect me with the crime, what will I say if the police talk to me, what if my wife, girlfriend, mother, or father finds out ..." These thoughts quickly led to the next stage.

Cover-up

In the *cover-up* stage you immediately attempted to hide the crime, either carefully with many elaborate precautions, or sloppily by leaving it to chance. Either way you wondered what to do next. The greater your fear, the more intensely you tried to *cover-up* your crime. If you had gotten away with it many times, you felt less fear and your need to *cover-up* was less intense.

You may have tried to *cover-up* your crime in several ways: some involved the victim, some the offender, and some the evidence. When you tried covering up by influencing the victim, you applied pressure: as subtle as making hints about how sad the victim's mother, father, boyfriend, or girlfriend would be if they found out; or as vicious as threatening to kill the victim if she or he told. When you pressured your victim, you probably thought, "Maybe I should give him something so he will shut up." "Maybe I can scare her so she'll keep quiet." "Maybe I can confuse her so she won't be believed." "Maybe I will take some photos of him and then I can tell him he is the guilty one who will be punished." "Maybe I should kill her so there will be no witnesses."

When you focused the *cover-up* on yourself, it usually involved some form of denial. You thought up alibis. You started lying to yourself, saying things like, "I wasn't the guilty one. I'm not responsible. I only did what she was asking for. How can I avoid that neighbor (or that neighborhood)?" You used all of your thinking defects during the *cover-up*.

When the *cover-up* involved evidence, you thought about how to manipulate the environment or friends and acquaintances so they would defend you if you got caught. You thought things like, "Maybe I should paint my car a different color. I'll think up a good lie about where I was and get my friends to believe it. Maybe I can leave town for a while. Maybe I should check and see if I left any footprints. Maybe I should dump the gun."

The *cover-up* stage deals with how you tried to make yourself feel and appear not guilty. But even when you were successful at hiding what happened, you often couldn't avoid the feelings of the next stage.

Shame and Guilt

Even when you managed to *cover-up* your crimes to others, inside you probably felt *shame and guilt*. *Shame* is a feeling of disgrace, dishonor, and betraying others, along with a fear of being singled out and ridiculed or excluded. You knew that when someone discovered what you had done, they would think less of you, and your relationship with them would be damaged. You couldn't count on them for support; they might hate and try to punish you. You may not have felt this emotion consciously, but your actions during the *cover-up* showed your sense of *shame*.

Guilt is a sense of responsibility for doing wrong. When you have an inner standard for behavior, you probably feel *guilt* because you are not measuring up to it when you are committing your assaults. Maybe your standard came from religion, or maybe a parent or relative showed you healthy moral values. Many offenders felt little obvious guilt during their crimes, especially those who spent years in prison, were numbed through violence, or who were so deeply into their deviancy that they had no access to a normal perspective. *Shame* and *guilt* usually link up with the next stage.

Self-hatred

Self-hatred comes out of your feelings of *shame and guilt*. You often tell yourself you are stupid, hateful, and worthless. When you feel worthless, you feel like no one else has any value either. When you feel worthless you don't care how important anyone else is. Often offenders wallow in this feeling. During the *Build-up* phase this feeling leads directly to more deviant behavior. Sometimes *self-hatred* is the link connecting the *Justification* phase and the *Build-up* phase, allowing the offender to go directly from committing one crime to committing another.

Your *self-hatred* shows in many ways: getting into fights, abusing others, self-destructive behavior, or total apathy. Fighting is a common symptom of hating yourself and others; wanting to be hurt, feeling proud of your scars, or displaying wounds may be a symptom of it. Self-destructive behavior also shows itself in many ways: cutting yourself, starving yourself, drinking yourself to death, or destroying things you love. Men who hate themselves don't succeed; they become failures in life. When things seem to be going well, they sabotage their own success, they do something to "screw it up." When you hate yourself you make promises that you'll change "somehow," and when you fail to fulfill those promises, your failure feeds your self-hate.

Promises, Promises

During the *self-hatred* phase you have some awareness of what a rotten thing you have done. You have some sense that what you have done is wrong. To make yourself feel better you make *promises* to yourself and others about how much better you will behave in the future. You say to yourself, "I *vow* before God never to do that again." "I *promise* that was the *last* time." "I'll *never* be weak like that again." "I've seen the light, I'll *never* touch her again." "I will *never* pick up another hitchhiker again." "I will *always* go to work every day on time and *never* waste so much time again." "I'll *never* have another drink."

You know it's a false and unrealistic promise—no matter how sincere—when you say words like, "I swear," "always," "never," "last," "really," "honest," and "this time for sure." Offenders are rarely able to keep these promises. They make you feel a little bit better or get you off the hook when someone confronts you. You may have been sincere at the time, but you quickly stash all these promises in a closed compartment in your mind and forget them.

Compartmentalizing

Another way you try to make yourself feel better is by putting your crime into a little compartment so you can pretend that it really isn't yours. You also *compartmentalize* the feelings of *self-hatred* and the attempts at *cover-up*. You stop thinking, "I'm bad," and begin thinking, "What I did was not so good, but as a whole I really am okay." You pretend it was really the alcohol or drugs that made you do it, ignoring why you use alcohol or drugs. Or you think that just dealing with your anger will fix everything else.

This kind of separation from the impact of your deviant sexual behavior allows you to feel like you are basically okay. During this phase, you think of positive things you've done that make up for the negative: "I helped my mother so I must really be okay." "I go to church every week, so my sins are forgiven." "I helped that person with their stuck car, so I really am a nice guy." "I gave my daughter a new teddy bear so I'm a good father." "I gave my wife $200 for her birthday, so I'm a good husband."

Compartmentalizing your crimes, putting them in little boxes separate from each other and from your sense of yourself, lets you focus only on the parts of your behavior you like. It lets you pretend that you're really a good guy, ignoring all the evidence to the contrary.

It is common for offenders in therapy to complain that therapy focuses only on the bad stuff. They want to tell their therapists about what is good in their lives. While being able to see the good in life is important, you have been using the "good" sides of yourself as a way of hiding the compartmentalized deviant side. You have to look at your deviant, destructive side clearly and realistically so you can change it.

Eventually you'll feel a difference between the good things you do to "look good"—to hide or in your own mind to make up for the pain you've caused—and genuinely kind, strong, moral, or "right" actions.

Thinking Defects

During the *Justification* phase you use different thinking defects from those of the *Build-up* phase. In the *Build-up* phase most of your thinking defects revolve around reasons why it is okay to be angry, depressed, or self-pitying. In the *Justification* phase your thinking defects center around ways to make yourself not seem so bad. For example, many offenders in prison begin thinking they have recovered. They decide that their crimes were less severe than the punishments they received, or that they are basically "nice guys," who just "made a mistake." They use these thinking defects to justify dropping out of treatment or filing appeals. "After all," they think, "it was the drugs that did it, not me." "It was a crazy period in my life, and now that it's over I don't have to worry about offending in the future."

You may also be using thinking defects during the *Justification* phase to make what you did to the victim seem not so bad: "I didn't really hurt him." "I only touched her." "She's a prostitute—she does it for a living." "She was asleep—she didn't know I did anything to her."

The thinking defects you use in the *Justification* phase help you overlook the fact that any state of mind that you have experienced in the past you will experience again. If you wanted to use drugs in the past, you will want to in the future. If you wanted to expose yourself in the past, you will want to again. If you wanted to rape in the past, you will have the same urge in the future. But you have a choice: you can help yourself choose not to act out by recognizing and being prepared for your worst impulses to tempt you again, especially when you're bored or under stress. You must plan interventions with these impulses so you will be able to stop them.

My Name Is _____ *and I'm a Sex Offender*
You probably resist the idea of labeling yourself as a sex offender. You're afraid that you'll get used to thinking about yourself that way and it will encourage you to act out. What happens is just the opposite.

As a sex offender you have a handicap, a weakness, that must be acknowledged for you to have any chance at living a full, satisfying, healthy life. Hiding your weakness from yourself and your family during your *Justification* phase is one sure way to set yourself up for a relapse.

Always think of yourself as a sex offender, the way an alcoholic always thinks of himself as an alcoholic, even when he hasn't had a drink in 20 years. By keeping the idea that you are a sex offender in mind, you keep the need for awareness and interventions in mind. It helps you prevent your own relapse into deviant behaviors.

Chapter 8 Assignments

∞ Do not write in this workbook ∞

29. The first goal of therapy is to help you not hurt any more victims. The justification phase of your cycle negatively affects your ability to develop empathy for your victim(s). List as many examples as you can in which you believe your justification phase prevented you from developing empathy for your victim(s), (e.g., I didn't hurt her, she didn't say "no", she has had sex before, etc.).

30. Write down ten (10) reasons why you as a sex offender might try to justify your criminal sexual behavior. How did those reasons affect you in your life?

31. Write down the ways you have tried to hide your deviant behavior. Consider how you tried to influence your victims, the environment, and yourself (remember, you can only say you did not try to hide your behavior if you went directly to the police and turned yourself in immediately).

32. Put the stages of the *Justification* phase in the order that makes sense for your cycle. The stages that were given included:

    Waking up, *Fear*, *Cover-up*, *Shame and Guilt*, *Self-hate*, *Promises*, and *Compartmentalizing*.

33. What promises, vows, or resolutions have you made in the past about your behavior? List at least ten (10).

34. Complete the diagram of your deviant cycle that you have been working on from assignments #12, #16, and #26 by including all aspects of your *Justification* phase in it. If you find that you have different facets of *Justification* from the ones that were mentioned in the text, feel free to put them in.

Review these assignments with your therapist and with your group. If you are working on your own, share the assignments with a friend or person you trust.

9.

The Secrets of the Cycle

BY NOW YOU ARE FAMILIAR with your deviant cycle. You understand about cycles, chains, and links. To make the cycle more useful to you it is important to understand the cycle's secrets. As you read about them, think about your own cycles. These examples will serve as guides for you to find the hidden ways that your cycle works.

Secret Beginnings

The cycle is not obvious. It is hidden. It never announces itself by saying, "Now I am starting. Watch out!" It starts simply, secretly, quietly, slowly.

Being able to recognize that you are in a cycle is the first step in recovery. By recognizing you are in a deviant cycle, you show yourself and others that you are ready to learn how to get out of it. Offenders usually say they are not in their deviant cycle, when asked, because they are not acting sexually deviant right now. You are afraid and don't want to be accused of doing wrong. You might be angry, but because anger feels so familiar you don't recognize it as part of your deviant cycle. Consider how Wally is doing.

Wally is not doing anything illegal or unusual. But as he continues blaming Ailene and not communicating with her, Wally's home life starts breaking down. Wally is in the beginnings of a deviant cycle, and if it continues, he will have more serious behavior problems. When Wally becomes aware of a cycle beginning, he can choose to intervene or ignore it. If he chooses to stop his cycle, he can sit down and talk with his wife or call his therapist. Once Wally knows that he is in a deviant cycle he can get out of it before he gets into more trouble.

Wally Worker

Wally felt under financial pressure. He chose to start working later than usual to earn more money. His wife, Ailene, was feeling overwhelmed and tired taking care of their three children and the house. Wally mentioned that he would be working later. He thought he would just do the extra work at his job and that Ailene would be pleased with the extra money. So Wally worked the extra hours and made more money, but he came home tense and tired. Wally figured that since he was working so much more at his job to "help the family," Ailene should do more of the home chores. Although he never discussed it with Ailene, Wally came home every day expecting her to take care of his chores around the house. Ailene was busy with her own work. She reminded him frequently about doing the yard work and his share of the laundry. Wally started feeling irritated and complained that she was "finding fault" with him. "After all," he thought, "look at all the extra work I'm doing at my job." He criticized Ailene, calling her "lazy" and "a bitch."

You're the Last to Know

You're always the last to know when you start sliding into a deviant cycle. Your family, friends, and co-workers are aware that something is going on with you. They may not call it a "deviant cycle," but they know that you don't look as good, act as pleasant, or feel as hopeful as you do at other times. Wally had a sense that something wasn't working, but didn't realize he was beginning a deviant cycle. Don doesn't have any idea that he might be in a deviant cycle.

> **Don Drinker**
>
> Don has gotten into the habit of having a couple of beers at lunchtime, a drink or two at night, and a couple of six-packs on the weekends. He knows that sometimes he drinks too much, but Don feels he has his drinking under control since he thinks that it doesn't interfere with his work. Occasionally when he goes to lunch he gets back to work late. But when Don is at work he tries to work extra hard to make up for his long lunches. He believes that no one knows how much he drinks and that everyone is satisfied with his performance.
>
> In reality, the entire crew is wondering why he is so hard to get along with. Don doesn't talk with them like he used to. He acts like something is on his mind and he doesn't want to be bothered. He is making more mistakes than usual and slowing the crew down. When someone tries to correct him he gets angry and tries to show them how he is not wrong. Recently Don's boss has started wondering whether or not to keep him on.

Many offenders who are in their deviant cycle think they are okay. If they notice anything wrong it looks to them like it is somebody else's problem. They think their wives and friends are being less patient, or the boss is picking on them more. When you don't know or don't admit you are in a deviant cycle you are more likely to stay in one.

Someone Else's Fault

One of the earliest signs of a deviant cycle is that you find reasons to blame everyone but yourself for your problems. The more reasonable it seems to you that someone else is at fault, the deeper you are in the cycle. When you are in a deviant cycle, you lose perspective on the two sides. You believe that what you are doing is totally the right thing and the other person is the cause of the problem. Any time you start blaming others for your problems without acknowledging that at least half the problem is your fault, you are either starting or are in a deviant cycle.

In life there are at least two sides to every situation. One side is that you are wrong and the other side is that someone else is wrong. Looking at two sides of the problem gives you the power to recognize that while you can't change other people, *you can change yourself.*

> **Ollie Ogler**
>
> Whenever Ollie went out he watched every woman he passed. When he saw a particularly attractive woman, he followed her and mentally undressed her, letting his mind dwell on the probable shape of her breasts.
>
> Frequently Ollie got into small "fender benders" with his car, usually nothing serious. Someone would open a car door in front of him or stop suddenly. Ollie would get out of the car and yell at the other driver for being so stupid. When Ollie's insurance rates were raised he was outraged. He went around cursing the "stupid insurance company," and raging about why the innocent drivers always have to pay for everyone else's recklessness.

Ollie is in a deviant cycle. If he had his mind on his driving, he could have avoided most of the accidents just by paying attention. Ollie was at least half at fault, but he blamed everyone else—from the other drivers to the insurance companies. When Ollie goes deeper into his cycle, he blames not only other drivers for his problems, but the women he is watching as well. Ollie says things like, "Women shouldn't dress so provocatively," or "She started flirting with me so it's her fault."

Alcoholics often blame their drinking on their families, friends, and employers. Rapists and child molesters usually claim that their victims caused the crime. The deeper you are in your deviant cycle, the more you blame others. This looks the same as when you lie and blame others to cover up the truth, but when you are in a deviant cycle (and not just lying), you, like Bill, *really believe* that others are at fault.

Bill Blamer
Bill, a long time child molester, was just arrested for another sexual crime. When interviewed about what happened he told his therapist, "Children always like me. I can't keep them away." "They like to play sexual games with me. I tell them to stop but they won't." "TV is the problem, there is too much sex on TV and it is corrupting the children." "Her father started it, he taught her to sit on his lap, so of course she wanted to sit on mine too." Bill says that he doesn't understand why he keeps getting into trouble.

"Stinking Thinking"

The deeper you are in your cycle, the more you repress your feelings. The more you repress your feelings, the more they distort your thinking. Your thinking defects rule your thoughts. When you are deep in your cycle, things that are really senseless seem reasonable. When you step outside your deviant cycle and look at what you have done, your "stinking thinking," like Paul's, becomes clear.

Paul Porn
Part of Paul's deviancy was buying pornography—lots of it. Paul spent thousands of dollars on different kinds of exotic pornographic video tapes. When he entered treatment, he got rid of his pornography. But recently Paul has begun to stop at the local quick market to look at pornographic magazines. Paul says to himself, "It's okay, I'll just look for a few minutes. I won't buy anything. I can stop anytime that I want to."

Paul is not thinking clearly as he begins his deviant cycle. The more Paul goes into his cycle, the more he will use thinking defects—rationalizing, minimizing, blaming others, and compartmentalizing—to justify his deviant behavior. As Paul uses more thinking defects, the more distorted his thinking will become and the deeper in the cycle he will go.

When you are in your deviant cycle, your thinking is distorted in specific ways. First, it impairs your ability to be rational and reasonable. You believe you are thinking well, but when you add two and two together you come up with five. Second, it interferes with your ability to think ahead. When you are in your cycle you can't relate to the long-term consequences of your behavior, focusing only on the short-term, pleasurable results. Saul's false sense of security is an example.

Saul Slider
Saul is in prison for the second time for molesting children. He knew the prison routine and how to slide by without too many problems. He felt good. His mind was calm. He got along well with the other prisoners. He had no problems with sex. When he thought about the future he assumed he would continue to feel good when he got out. He thought, "Prison is so bad that if I can make it in here, I know I can get by on the outside." Saul felt that he had no sexual problems. He figured he was smart and could get along anywhere. Saul repeatedly told himself that what had happened was just a "bad mistake." He got involved in therapy so it would look good in his file, but didn't think he really needed any help. He slid through it, bored with the process.

Saul obviously has big problems. No sex offender goes to prison twice (or even once) unless he has serious problems. But because his thinking is distorted, he doesn't realize how big his problems are. Saul thinks that because he is managing well in prison, he will manage well outside, even though his history on the outside counters that fantasy. Because his thinking is disturbed, he can't see that he needs to make a number of personal changes to prepare himself for his future. He is focusing on today's calm instead of preparing himself for tomorrow's challenges.

Holey Memory

When you are in your deviant cycle, your memory is rusty, full of holes. You don't remember the pain, humiliation, and despair of your deviant cycles in the past. Events associated with negative emotions (like fear and anger) are a vague blur. By forgetting, like Fred, you are setting yourself up for failure.

> ### Fred Forgetful
> Fred got a 20-year prison sentence for raping a young girl who was left in his care. When Fred was arrested he felt terrible about his crime. He pled guilty without trying too hard to defend himself. For the first year Fred was deeply depressed, felt dreadful, and knew he needed help. By the second year, when Fred thought about his past, it didn't seem so bad—certainly not equal to the 20 years that he got. He still remembered the details of his crime and felt the intense excitement that he had while committing it. Fred forgot the horror and despair that he felt when he was arrested. He forgot how unhealthy he must have been to commit his crime. He dropped out of treatment saying, "I'm really okay. I can do what I need on my own."

Steve also has *holey memory*.

> ### Steve Sloshed
> Steve uses his weekly pay to drink all weekend. By Monday he feels awful, broke, hung over, and embarrassed by what he has done. Bill collectors are calling and visiting him at work. His heat is being turned off, the phone company is about to disconnect his phone, and Steve's ex-wife is trying to garnish his wages because he hasn't paid his child support. But by Friday he forgets how bad he felt on Monday and thinks he will feel still better if he has a few drinks this weekend too. On Monday he knows he needs help. By Friday he says, "It's not such a big problem, I can handle it by myself."

These two men forget their out-of-control behavior, the loneliness, despair, and rage. They don't think about the future. And without long-term help, both of them will stay in their cycles, repeating their destructive behaviors, feeling bad, hurting others, getting caught, losing jobs, going to jail.

The Cycle Spins You

When the deviant cycle is established "it" begins to live your life for you. By the time your deviant cycle is controlling your life, it does not matter how the cycle got started. It becomes like a forest fire. The more area that the fire covers, the greater the risk for more fires. Once the deviant cycle gets started it continues and gets larger. Maintaining the cycle becomes your life, like Francis's cycle became his life.

> ### Francis Flasher
> Francis gets up in the morning and feels tense. On his way to work he gets sidetracked and drives around looking for someone he can flash (expose himself) to. Once Francis starts his cycle, he drives for hours to find the right victim in the right place. His boss has told him that if he misses one more day of work without a doctor's note, he'll be fired. His wife is upset because he's so preoccupied and distant. He is losing his marriage, his job, and his self-respect but Francis can't seem to stop his compulsive behavior.

The cycle seems like it has a will of its own. When Francis is deeply in it, his life is out of control. He begins to live for the cycle. Exposing becomes more important to him than his wife, his children, his job, or his self-respect. Because his cycle is so firmly established, only a crisis can break him out of it: he might lose his job, his wife might leave, or he could get arrested. Any of these crises might help him stop, but without intervention and treatment, the cycle comes around again and again.

The Cycle Feeds Itself

The cycle has a life of its own. When you are in a deviant cycle your mind is not working well; the things you think you are doing to get out of your cycle often make the cycle worse. Drug addicts often use drugs to escape from their pain and boredom. The more they use drugs, the more pain and boredom they feel and the more they want to use drugs. Felix's cycle just keeps coming around.

Felix Fondler

Felix is afraid that he will be found out. He has masturbated a neighbor boy and is worried that the kid may tell his parents. Felix has discovered that when he is masturbating he does not feel anxious. Felix's anxiety is so great that he starts masturbating to get some relief. While Felix is masturbating he starts to think about how exciting sex with a young boy would be. Felix feels better as long as he is thinking about sex. That afternoon Felix is asked to babysit a neighbor child. He feels tremendous distress about what he might do. Because he feels so much distress, he starts thinking about sex to make himself feel better. The more he thinks about sex the more he wants to babysit.

Felix feels tremendous anxiety. Anxiety (like anger, self-hatred, and other stressful feelings) fuels the deviant cycle. The more anxiety Felix feels, the more he gets involved in sexual deviance. The more he's involved in sexual deviance, the more anxiety he feels—a self-perpetuating cycle. It is hard to stop it without disclosure, and that idea produces more anxiety. Your anxiety overcomes your will to resist the deviant behavior. However, the reason for your deviant behavior is to get some relief from your anxiety and distress. Once the cycle is well established, anxiety is unnecessary: the need to feel excited or powerful may fuel the cycle.

High Speed Cycles

Your cycle does not stay the same: it gets worse and moves faster. Remember Horny Hank's story from Chapter Seven? His cycle got more and more intense until it got him into trouble with the law.

Your deviant cycle probably started slowly and got progressively more deviant and compulsive. The longer you let it run, the stronger your cycle becomes and the greater your deviancy. Each time the cycle goes around, each time Hank picks up a prostitute, the easier it is for him to do it again. Maybe you pick up hitchhikers to rape, or expose yourself, or molest children. Whatever your deviancy, the more you do it the easier it is to do again.

A Wheel within a Wheel

You can have more than one deviant cycle. For example, you may have cycles of alcohol and sex, anger and sex, or alcohol and depression. When you have more than one deviant cycle, the cycles tend to make each other worse. If your cycle is alcohol and depression, the more alcohol that you drink, the more depressed you feel. The more depressed you feel, the more alcohol you drink. Roy's anger and deviant sexual cycles are turning into rape.

Roy Raper

Roy's anger cycle starts when he is afraid of being seen as incompetent and weak. He tries to compensate for his feelings of insecurity and inadequacy by being a tough guy. Roy has learned that if he gets angry quickly, violently, and frequently, people around him never know that he is quivering with fear inside.

Roy also has a sexual cycle. He is addicted to sex and will sacrifice anything for a "good lay." His two deviant cycles can combine to make his problems worse. Lately, Roy has learned that if he has sex when he is angry, his womanfriend gets scared and acts weak and vulnerable. Roy soon discovers that he can have good sex and feel very powerful at the same time. When his womanfriend doesn't submit, Roy enjoys overpowering her. Now, in order to have what he considers "good sex," he *has* to beat her up and force her to have sex. His behavior has developed into rape.

When an individual has two or more deviant cycles, the cycles can feed one another. In Roy's case the more angry he became, the more deviant his sexual desires were. The more deviant his sexual desires, the more he acted out his anger. When you have two deviant cycles, you make both stronger each time one of them is active. It is twice as hard to stop two deviant cycles.

Lies, Secrets, and Silence

When you are in your deviant cycle you lie. You lie to your therapist, your parole officer, your family, your victim, and yourself. It is impossible to be involved with deviant behavior and tell the truth. The longer you let your cycle run, the more lies you have to tell. Lies generate more lies: lying once leads to lying twice. Staying in the cycle requires you to lie and hide your behavior. You become secretive, and secrecy makes you feel powerful. When you choose not to lie and hide your behavior, you break the deviant cycle. You are probably afraid that the cost of being honest is too high. But as Larry found out, the price of honesty is cheap compared to the cost of deviancy.

Larry Liar

Larry is a rapist who is in therapy trying to "go straight." While at a car repair shop he noticed a series of Hustler centerfolds on the wall and got aroused. When his therapist asked Larry if he had seen any pornography that week, Larry lied and said no. Afterwards he thought, "That was easy." A few days later he was in a video store, saw an R-rated movie with a sexual theme and impulsively rented it. Lying to himself Larry thought, "This doesn't have anything to do with rape." He watched it and got turned on.

Larry began having flashes of doing another rape. When his therapist asked Larry if he was having any deviant fantasies, Larry lied again: "I'm okay," he lied, "I'm staying out of risky situations, and I'm not doing anything bad." But Larry had started buying pornographic magazines again. His thoughts and emotions are beginning to get out of control. Larry is afraid that if his therapist finds out about the flashes and what he is thinking and doing, he will report Larry to the parole officer.

Larry pretends he is okay by avoiding his therapist. He goes to group but does not participate. When he is asked a direct question, he lies to make himself look strong and good. But Larry has been checking women out regularly and drives by their houses. He knows he is in trouble. He has lied so much before that he is afraid of being found out and punished. He also lies to his therapist about being afraid, and about how being afraid makes him angry. A few weeks later he commits another rape.

When you are deep in a cycle you must be lying to someone. Lies keep the cycle going. You must lie to yourself and others over and over in order to work yourself into a mind-state to commit a crime. The truth will break a cycle every time.

Illusions of Control

When the earliest sign of a deviant cycle starts you say, "I'm in control. I can stop when I want to." This is an illusion, a pipe dream, a thinking defect. As soon as your deviant cycle gets going, you stop wanting to quit, and your deviant cycle begins to control you. Perry's story shows what happens when you slip back into old patterns of behavior.

Perry Powertrip

Perry has beaten his wife a few times and recently got into a fight with a neighbor. He got into therapy and was learning how to control his anger. After a few months he felt confident that he was in charge of his life and that his anger was under control.

One day Perry and his wife began arguing. Perry felt that he was losing and he didn't want to. He knew that it was dangerous for him to allow himself to be angry, but Perry said to himself, "I can handle my anger, I'm in control of it now." He decided to let just a little of his anger out to show her who was the boss. He thought, "I can turn my anger on and off when I want to." Perry let himself get angry. He started to feel powerful as his wife became intimidated. As his anger grew, Perry began beating his wife, and it felt so good that he didn't want to stop. Perry battered his wife until she was unconscious; he got scared and called the ambulance to take her to the hospital. She is pressing charges for assault, and he's awaiting trial.

Carl Crapper

Carl is a coprophilic, compulsively sexually turned on by feces (shit). On bad days he cruises the bathrooms of the building where he works looking for feces left in the toilets. When Carl finds some he collects it and uses it to masturbate with. On his bad days he knows he has a big problem and thinks about finding a therapist and getting some help. Carl even found a clinic that specializes in sexual problems and made an appointment.

But on his good days or weeks Carl does not engage in his deviant behavior; he stays at his desk and works continuously. When he is feeling good he says to himself, "I've almost got this thing under control. I don't need to tell anyone about this." Then Carl cancels his appointment. This cycle has been going on for years.

Rollercoasters

The cycle changes. It goes up and down in intensity, you have "good days" and "bad days." Even when you are deep in your cycle your thinking defects help you find evidence that you don't need any outside help. But just because your cycle is less intense right now, doesn't mean you're not in it: when you are doing deviant behavior, using thinking defects, or repressing your feelings, you are in a deviant cycle. Carl is always up and down in his cycle.

Even when you are deep in your cycle, there are good days and bad days. If you have big problems, feeling good is fine, but it doesn't mean you've got the answer. You help keep your deviant cycle alive and well when you take credit for random good days or weeks. When you use these times as evidence that you are not out of control, you are burying yourself in your cycle.

The Willpower Delusion

Another delusion that keeps the deviant cycle going is thinking, "I can do it by myself if I just have enough willpower." Willpower alone won't work. You have probably tried it many times before. How many New Year's resolutions have you kept?

When you are in a deviant cycle you are isolated, a kind of loner. You might not be alone, but you are so wrapped up in your own thoughts, feelings, and desires, that no one else can have much effect on you. "I can do it by myself," shows that you think your problems are unique to you, that you are special and unusual. You don't want anyone else to know about them because you're afraid they'll think that you are weak or sick.

The classic image of a loner is the tough cowboy who can take care of himself and needs nothing from anyone else. But the "Marlboro Man" is an advertising myth; everyone needs help. When you think you don't need help, you're deep into the *"One-and-Only"* thinking defect, just like Lance.

Lance Loner

Lance has been sexual with his 12-year-old daughter for months. Last week while his wife was at the beach with the kids, he watched a program on TV about incest. He knew that incest was damaging his daughter. Lance made up his mind never to touch his daughter sexually again. He thought about getting some help, but he knew that Children's Protective Services would get involved. The idea that the agency would "interfere" with him and his family made Lance angry. He said to himself, "She's my daughter, it's my problem, and I can take care of things myself." Lance thought that he could fix the problem and make things better for his daughter "somehow." That night Lance sneaked into his daughter's room again for "one last time."

Willpower does not stop you from getting into your deviant cycle. As one offender said, "Have you ever tried willpower with diarrhea?" You, and everyone else in a deviant cycle, need outside help from friends, family, social service agencies, and counselors. Like all of us, you need help at times. Strength is acknowledging your weaknesses and being man enough to say it without shame.

Chapter 9 Assignments

∞ **Do not write in this workbook** ∞

35. In this chapter there are eleven (11) examples of the hidden ways your deviant cycle works. Write down at least seven (7) that apply to your cycle.

36. For each of the hidden ways you picked in assignment #35 write out an example that shows how this hidden way has operated in your cycle.

37. Now review your deviant cycle from assignments #12, #16, and #26 and see if you can add in any of the hidden links, thoughts, chains, etc. When you have finished with the total cycle, make a copy for yourself and turn one copy in to your therapist.

Review these assignments with your therapist and with your group. If you are working on your own, share the assignments with a friend or person you trust.

10.
Interrupting Your Cycle: Basic Interventions

THE REASON YOU ARE READING and learning about the deviant cycle is to stop it at its very first sign. There are many ways of intervening in your cycle—all part of relapse prevention—but none of them will work unless you want them to, *unless you want to stop your deviant behavior and remain crime-free*.

In Chapter Eleven of our first workbook, *Who Am I?*, we discussed relapse prevention in detail. You learned that there are no *cures* for sexual deviancy. No matter how strongly you feel that you will not commit another sexual crime, when you make the wrong choices and indulge in distorted thinking, feelings, and behavior, your sexual problems return.

You also learned that the essence of relapse prevention is anticipating and avoiding risk situations, and making escape plans to fall back on. Identifying the signs and symptoms of a possible risk situation allows you to plan ahead of time how you will respond, like Patrick did.

Patrick Planner
Patrick has molested children in the past, but is now in treatment and wants to stop. He needs to go shopping and knows he might find lots of children in the mall. Before he leaves for the mall, he thinks about what he'll do if that happens. "First," he thinks, "I'll go in the morning while the kids are in school. Then I won't go near the arcade. And if those two things don't work and there are kids at the mall, I'll leave and call a friend. Then I'll put it in my log and talk it over with my group."

In this chapter we introduce some of the common approaches to relapse prevention. The next workbook in this series, *How Can I Stop? Breaking My Deviant Cycle*, is devoted to helping you learn and use these techniques and others. If possible, find a therapist and a treatment program to work with so you can get more detailed and direct guidance. If there is any conflict between what your therapist says and what you read in the workbook, listen primarily to your therapist; after all, he or she knows you and your situation best.

Awareness is the first step toward stopping a deviant cycle. By reading and doing the assignments in this book, you have already taken that first step. The more you learn about how you think and act, the better equipped you are to intervene in your deviant behavior.

Recognizing how you act under stress is one kind of awareness that helps you break your cycle early. Knowing when the stress and increasing tension of your deviant cycle start, how to reduce them, and how to promote relaxation is an essential part of recovery. The better equipped you are to handle stress, the less likely you are to repeat your deviant cycle as a way of dealing with that stress.

Awareness helps you change your behavior. Behavioral science has shown that having enough awareness of a behavior to be able to count and track it reduces the occurrence of that behavior. For example, it has been shown that if a person wishes to stop smoking, counting each cigarette and becoming aware of each step in the chain of smoking reduce the number of cigarettes smoked.

However, awareness alone will not stop a smoker from smoking. He needs motivation and some specific interventions to aid him. The same is true in stopping your deviant cycle. While awareness is the first step, you must also be strongly motivated to use specific interventions to keep you crime-free and change your whole style of living to maintain your recovery process with some of the general interventions listed below.

Specific Intervention Techniques

When you are willing to be honest there are several techniques that may help you stop your deviant cycle. Three are described briefly below: two you can use on your own; the other requires help from a skilled therapist. Again, if you have the option, be sure to get into a treatment program so that the program staff can aid you in developing an intervention plan that fits your needs.

1. **Thought-stopping:** As you remember, the *Build-up* phase of the cycle often starts with fantasy. Imagining a sexual encounter or fantasizing about getting even with someone are typical ways that the Build-up starts. You form links in your deviant chain from these thoughts and the emotional reactions that follow. Stopping fantasies is an important ability for recovery.

To use *thought-stopping*, first identify the thoughts you need to stop—your sexually deviant or violent fantasies. You must be specific and clear about exactly which thoughts you want to stop. It won't work to say you want to stop "deviant thoughts," because your thinking defects won't let you recognize them as deviant. You might want to stop "sexual thoughts about children" or "images of sexual bondage."

Every time you notice the target thoughts coming into your mind say, "STOP!" It works best if you can say it out loud, but since you may feel weird about letting your friends hear you saying "STOP!" all the time, you can do it in your mind. As soon as you have said, "STOP!" you must replace the deviant thought with a new appropriate one. Here's how Stan dealt with his deviant thoughts.

> **Stan Stopper**
> Stan was a rapist. He had flashes of sex with his victim that he couldn't get out of his mind. They were sexually arousing even though he didn't want them to be. So Stan decided to use a thought-stopping technique. Whenever a violent thought came into his mind, he said, "QUIT IT!" and snapped a rubber band on his wrist. Then he said a short prayer, "Lord help me to respect and cherish this person." After he did this consistently for several months, Stan noticed that the fantasies were not so intense and they occurred less and less often until he finally stopped having them at all.

There are several important points in Stan's example. He used a replacement thought appropriate to *him*. Stan was a strongly religious person; for him prayer was the best thing to keep violent sexual thoughts from returning. When you choose replacement thoughts pick something *important to you*, a personal aspiration that opposes the fantasy. Select a replacement thought you can use consistently, since the intervention must be immediate and automatic. It takes too long to try to think of something appropriate each time.

Stan snapped a rubber band looped around his wrist when he said "QUIT IT!" This variation of the technique helps him interrupt his violent thoughts more definitely. Unless Stan intervenes, his sexual arousal acts as a reward for his deviant thoughts. Snapping the rubber band really catches his attention (pulling him out of his automatic thought chain), helps him replace his deviant thoughts, and by interrupting his arousal does not reward him for having violent sexual thoughts.

Many alternative techniques can be used in lieu of the rubber band: pinching yourself, biting your lip, and breaking an ammonia capsule are all aversive techniques that discourage the continuation of your deviant fantasy. Do not use these techniques to punish yourself; they are just to catch your attention briefly so you can interrupt your deviant thoughts. Using aversive techniques to punish yourself causes more problems and feeds your deviant cycle by making you feel bad. If possible, consult with a therapist about the appropriate use of these techniques.

2. **Sexual Arousal Conditioning:** Learning to change your sexual arousal requires working with an experienced therapist who is skilled in conditioning techniques and the use of the penile plethysmograph. The plethysmograph is an objective way to measure sexual arousal. During this evaluation you are alone in a private room. You place a circular gauge (like a rubber band) around your penis. You hear a series of audiotapes or see videotapes of sexual scenarios. As you respond sexually to the material, the plethysmograph measures the degree of your arousal and helps the therapist determine the proper course of treatment for you.

Once your therapist determines exactly what deviant material you are aroused to, you can be trained not to respond to it by a process called conditioning. An image that is sexually arousing to you is presented. As you begin to respond with your usual arousal and pleasurable excitement, an aversive stimulus is given: a foul smell, an anxiety-producing scene, a loud or unpleasant sound, or occasionally a mild electric shock. The pleasant excitement associated with sexual arousal to an inappropriate image is replaced by the unpleasant feeling. This replacement of pleasant feelings with unpleasant ones enables many men to disrupt their deviant arousal (you can even learn to self-administer an aversive smell).

3. **Covert Sensitization:** This is a sophisticated form of sexual arousal conditioning. The purpose is to replace deviant but pleasurable excitement with images of realistic and unpleasant consequences. For example, if you are sexually aroused to young children, you might replace the arousing pictures in your mind with images of the police arresting you, or your wife walking in while you were molesting a child.

While the following example describes a simple form of covert sensitization, there are other more complex ways of using this technique. Some involve explicit sexual scenarios, complex interweaving of images, or taping of the story lines. If you are not working with a therapist, follow the example below and keep it simple.

A. *Identify* your deviant arousal. It may be to violent sex, children, exposing yourself, peeping, or other sexual activity.

B. *Run a movie* through your mind of what your typical set-up activity would look like. Stop at the point of sexual involvement. Do not fantasize about the sexual activity itself. For example, you might see a child in the park. Imagine that you are going to talk to the child. See yourself making friends with the child and then talking him or her into going into the bushes with you to "play a game." Or if you are a rapist, you might see a hitchhiker: imagine stopping and picking her up, talking to her about sex, and then turning off onto a deserted road. Again, STOP before you begin to think of specific sexual activity.

C. As the movie is running thorough your mind, *say "STOP!"* to yourself at the point where you would begin the sexual activity. Then *imagine a scary scene* that could be a consequence of your deviant action. For example, if you are imagining molesting a child, you might see the child's angry father suddenly appear, or the police grabbing you and handcuffing you. If you are imagining a rape you might imagine your mother and father or the minister of your church watching you or a police car's flashing lights coming on behind you while you have the woman in your car.

Allow the aversive imagery to develop in your mind until you *feel anxiety or fear*. Sometimes a therapist will assist this aversive feeling with a noxious odor or a loud, startling sound. *Repeat* this procedure *three times a day* for each deviant behavior.

D. After you have done three repetitions, *replace* the aversive scene *with a positive scene* that would be possible if you did not do a sexual crime: for example, having dinner with your wife, taking your family to church, getting married, being promoted in a job, etc.

When you use covert sensitization it is important to see the pictures in your mind. Play a movie of the scenes that you are working with; don't just think the words. Try to describe a scene with as much detail as possible, as Ron has done in the example below.

> **Recovering Ron**
> **Identifying his arousal problem:**
> I have arousal to young boys about 10 years old.
>
> **Running a movie about his set-up for the sexual crime; stopping before anything sexual occurs:**
> I am out for a walk. I pass by an elementary school. It is about 3:00 pm and I know that the kids will be coming out very soon. I wait on a bench playing with a remote-controlled car. Soon the children come out of school. Several 9- and 10-year-old boys come around and timidly watch me. I see one boy who is fresh, young, has blond hair and blue eyes. He is very attractive. I ask several of the boys if they want to try driving the car. They say yes! I put my arms around them and "help" them to control it. The last one that I ask is the blond boy I've spotted. I tell him that I have to go home and ask him if he wants to drive the car and come with me. I follow the blond boy and watch his cute body as we walk. I get rid of the other children after a block or two. When we get home I tell the blond boy that I have other cars inside and ask him if he would like to try them out. He says yes and follows me inside ...
>
> **Saying "STOP!"; imagining a scary scene; feeling anxiety:**
> STOP! Suddenly I see the police pull up outside my house. They charge up the steps and pound on the door. I know that I am caught. The police come in and find the 10-year-old boy in the house. They take him aside and ask him questions. They arrest me, put me in the police car, and take me to the station. There they book me and call my parole officer, who calls my wife. I know that I will be in jail for years, my wife will divorce me, and my legal expenses will cost every cent I have. I feel so ashamed and humiliated. I'm scared about what will happen. *(Repeat three times.)*
>
> **Replacing with a positive scene:**
> I see the elementary school and immediately turn down another street. I walk straight home and record my risk situation so I can tell my group. My wife comes in and asks if I'd like to go out for some ice cream. I say yes! I feel good that I have succeeded in avoiding temptation. My wife notices that I am happy and says how much she enjoys being with me when I'm in this mood.

When you read the third in our series of Sex Offenders' Studies, *How Can I Stop? Breaking My Deviant Cycle*, you will have even more tools to make healthy changes in your life.

General Interventions

1. **Getting Honest:** The most important way you can intervene in your deviant cycle is being honest. Being honest with yourself, your friends, your family, and your potential victims is the quickest way to break a cycle.

In the *Build-up* phase dishonesty about your fantasies, plans, and reasons for anger and depression keep your cycle going. Telling one (honest) person what you are thinking of doing sexually will interrupt your plans. The *Acting-out* phase is based on dishonesty and manipulation. When you are honest with your potential victim and with yourself about the consequences, you can stop acting out.

The *Justification* phase is devoted to hiding and minimizing the truth; it is totally disrupted when you are honest. Being honest with yourself and everyone you meet is the first condition to healing. In the *Pretend-normal* phase you are not honestly looking at your life and problems. You are pretending that what you have done is not affecting you now.

2. **Fantasy Logs:** A fantasy can be a daydream, a momentary flash, or any other kind of imaginative thought that involves your deviancy. Your fantasy can begin when you notice a woman's figure, see a child, catch sight of an advertisement using women or children in sexually suggestive poses, or think, "Wouldn't it be nice if ..." One fantasy leads to another and another and another. Carrying a notebook in your pocket and logging your fantasies help you become aware how often you are influenced by your fantasies. In the notebook you would write down where and when you fantasize, your emotional state, your reaction to the fantasy (including whether or not you masturbated), and how you intervened to stop your fantasy. The log becomes a written record that not only increases your awareness of when fantasies begin, but also reminds you of the interventions that worked and lets you learn from your successes.

3. **Anger Management:** In general, anger fuels the deviant cycle. Stopping the habit of anger and identifying underlying feelings is an effective way to break a cycle. Breaking the habit of anger has two main parts. The first part involves stopping the *immediate experience* of anger. The second part concerns changing your sensitivity to the *triggers* you use to get angry.

You can interrupt the immediate habit of anger by noticing and writing down the "getting angry" signs in your body, in your mind, and in your emotions. Once you are aware of the signs of getting angry, notice and write down where and at what you get angry. After you have become aware of where and when you usually get angry, you can plan ways of stopping your angry reactions, like using a *time-out*, a specific series of behaviors that interrupt your angry reactions. A time-out is a short cooling-off period that allows you to work off some of your angry energy in nondestructive ways so you can think about why you feel angry and talk about it later.

Long-term anger management means identifying and expressing the feelings that underlie your anger, learning the habit of intervention, and stopping your angry thoughts.

4. **Social and Communication Skills Training:** Most sex offenders have difficulty with personal communication. They do not know how to talk about their intimate feelings and have trouble sharing what is really on their minds. *Communication training* teaches you how to listen, how to give feedback, how to take criticism, and how to share personal feelings. *Social skills training* involves learning about socially appropriate behaviors and limits: for example, learning what is appropriate dating behavior for healthy people or how to talk with women socially.

5. **Autobiography:** Writing your autobiography teaches you about your history, how you got to where you are now, and the consequences of your deviancy. Writing down in detail what you remember from your earliest days to the present gives you a sense of how your life is connected. The process of writing it down and being able to look it over several times often helps motivate offenders to make new choices from now on.

6. **Countering Thinking Defects:** Changing the thinking defects you use in your deviant cycle involves four steps: *identifying* the thinking defects you use (see Chapter Three); *writing out* what's wrong with each thinking defect and what the truth is; *noticing and countering* your thinking defects when you start "hearing" them in your mind; and *practicing* this technique over and over until the new thoughts become your normal ones.

7. **Assertiveness Training:** Acquiring the mutual skills of personal power and respect for others involves learning the difference between being passive, being assertive, and being aggressive. Assertiveness training teaches you how to speak your mind appropriately, express your needs, and get your needs met without stepping on or hurting others. Many child molesters, exhibitionists, and voyeurs need assertiveness training. You can learn how to observe your own behavior and practice being assertive rather than passive or aggressive until you gradually drop your passive/aggressive stance.

8. **Victim Empathy Training:** All sex offenders need to understand the short- and long-term effects of their sexual crimes on victims. This understanding motivates many offenders to stop victimizing others. Working on any sexual trauma you may have experienced as a child by using movies, tapes, stories, books, and confrontations by victims teaches you about the devastating effects of sex abuse and of your behavior.

Maintaining Your Nondeviant Life

When you have begun to change and are living in the community, you will need help, education, and support in many areas of your life to maintain and continue your recovery. For example, sex-offender treatment programs help you replace your deviant sexuality with a *positive sexuality* that promotes mutual respect, nurturing, and pleasure between partners.

In *recreational therapy*, also available through sex-offender treatment programs, you learn healthy ways to enjoy yourself. When you stop participating in activities that promote your deviancy, you need to replace the old behaviors with new skills, including how to spend free time, how to enjoy healthy excitement, and how to get your social needs met in a healthy way.

Finding *social support groups* that encourage honesty and promote mutual support is essential to breaking your old deviant cycles. Groups such as Alcoholics Anonymous, Narcotics Anonymous, Sexual Addicts Anonymous or Sexaholics Anonymous are all useful resources for an offender who wants to assure and maintain his recovery. Participating actively in such groups also interrupts your tendency to withdraw from people when you're starting a deviant cycle.

Chapter 10 Assignment

∞ Do not write in this workbook ∞

38. By now you have completed your deviant cycle. Now go back over each step of it and insert a possible intervention to help you stop the cycle. Consult with your therapist and friends to make sure that your interventions are reasonable and appropriate. You should find at least twelve (12) places to intervene in your cycle.

Review this assignment with your therapist and with your group. If you are working on your own, share the assignment with a friend or person you trust.

Congratulations!

Understanding the architecture of your deviant cycle is a major step toward breaking your cycle. By completing this workbook and your homework assignments, you have equipped yourself with a strong tool to break the links and chains of your deviant cycle. By understanding how today's actions influence you next week or next year, you can take real control over your life, making positive choices for the future and leaving the old "victim of circumstances" identity behind. The map you now have of your deviant cycle is a plan for change. You can make real change now that you understand how your decisions are influenced by what you do, think, and feel. Understanding how you go wrong gives you an awareness of how to go right.

Again, congratulations!

Recommended Readings

Who Am I And Why Am I In Treatment? by Robert Freeman-Longo & Laren Bays (1988). The Safer Society Press, P.O. Box 340, Brandon, VT 05733. $12.00.

How Can I Stop? Breaking My Deviant Cycle by Laren Bays, Robert Freeman-Longo, & Diane Montgomery-Logan (1990). Safer Society Press, PO Box 340, Brandon, VT 05733-0340. $12.00.

Men & Anger by Murray Cullen & Robert E. Freeman-Longo (1995). The Safer Society Press, P.O. Box 340, Brandon, VT 05733. $12.00.

Empathy & Compassionate Action: Issues and Exercises by Robert Freeman-Longo, Laren Bays & Euan Bear (1996). The Safer Society Press, PO Box 340, Brandon, VT 05733-0340. $12.00.

Man-to-Man: When Your Partner Says No—Pressured Sex & Date Rape by Scott Allen Johson (1992). Safer Society Press, PO Box 340, Brandon, VT 05733-0340. $6.50.

Adults Molested as Children: A Survivor's Manual for Women & Men by Euan Bear with Peter T. Dimock (1988). Safer Society Press, PO Box 340, Brandon, VT 05733-0340. $12.95.

Men Surviving Incest by T. Thomas (1989). Launch Press, P.O. Box 5629, Rockville, MD 20855. $7.95.

Surviving with Serenity: Daily Meditations for Incest Survivors by T. Thomas (1990). Health Communications, Inc., 3201 S.W. 15th Street, Deerfield Beach, FL 33442. $6.95.

Secret Feelings and Thoughts by Rosemary Narimanian (1990). Philly Kids Play It Safe, 1650 Arch Street, 17th Fl., Suite 1700, Philadelphia, PA 19103. $10.00.

Victims No Longer: Men Recovering from Incest by Mike Lew (1988). Harper & Row, 10 East 53rd Street, New York, NY 10022. $14.95.

Male Survivors: 12-Step Recovery Program for Survivors of Childhood Sexual Abuse by Timothy L. Sanders (1991). The Crossing Press, Freedom, CA 95019. $12.95.

Macho: Is That What I Really Want? by Py Bateman & Bill Mahoney (1986). Youth Education Systems, Box 223, Scarborough, NY 10510. $4.75.

You Don't Have to Molest That Child by Timothy A. Smith (1987). National Committee for Prevention of Child Abuse (NCPCA), 332 S. Michigan Avenue, Suite 950, Chicago, IL 60604-4357. $2.00.

The Safer Society Press
PO Box 340
Brandon, VT 05733-0340
(802) 247-3132

Order Form

Shipping Address:

Date: _____

☐ **Please send a catalog.**

Name and/or Agency _____

Address _____

City _____ State _____ Zip _____

Billing Address (if different from shipping address):

Address _____

City _____ State _____ Zip _____

Daytime Phone (_____) _____

P.O. No. _____

Qty	Title	Unit Price	Total Cost

Make checks payable to:
SAFER SOCIETY PRESS

Sub Total _____

VT residents add sales tax _____

Shipping _____

US FUNDS ONLY. All prices subject to change without notice.

TOTAL _____

Mail to:

Add 8% to all orders
for shipping & handling

Bulk order discounts available
Rush Orders – add $10.00

Safer Society Press
PO BOX 340 • BRANDON, VT 05733-0340
PHONE: (802) 247-3132